GOD ON EARTH

Spiritual Messages and Life Lessons

KAREN HEUMANN

BALBOA.
PRESS
A DIVISION OF HAY HOUSE

ISBN: 978-1-4525-6138-7 (sc)
ISBN: 978-1-4525-6140-0 (hc)
ISBN: 978-1-4525-6139-4 (e)

Library of Congress Control Number: 2012919612

Balboa Press books may be ordered through booksellers or by contacting:

Balboa Press
A Division of Hay House
1663 Liberty Drive
Bloomington, IN 47403
www.balboapress.com
1-(877) 407-4847

Printed in the United States of America

Balboa Press rev. date: 10/19/2012

To everyone who believes in angels.
To my children, Eric, Alec, Casey, and
Karrson, my heart.
To my husband, Mike, my rock, my foundation.
To my friends for acceptance, spirited debate,
love and consideration.
To everyone who ever said you can, you are,
you will be, you wouldn't want to anyway.
To the manufacturers of vitamins.
Thank you.

TABLE OF CONTENTS

Ask in prayer, trust in the answer.

Matthew 7:7 Ask and it will be given to you; seek and you will find; knock and the door will be opened to you.

GOD ON EARTH
SPIRITUAL MESSAGES AND LIFE LESSONS

For as long as I can remember, I was told that "God is all around us." And, both with and without evidence, I have held to that belief for my entire life. There are times when that time-held belief is exemplified; those times when the presence of God is palpable. This book of spiritual messages and life lessons is about those times.

Sometimes life throws us curveballs. This book includes personal stories about survival, struggle, lessons learned, how it is all much easier when I ask for help in prayer, and a recognition that sometimes, a lot of times, I am not even asking the right question- or listening to the answer. And, more often than not, I get many answers or a larger answer than anticipated, something meaningful to more than just that moment, to larger life questions, more fundamental, defining, and integral to living itself.

I Chronicles 16:11 Seek the LORD and His strength; Seek His face continually.

I used to think God's presence that uplifting feeling I experienced while singing at church, that collective outpouring of impassioned love, chorus of voices praising, worshipping, soulful, longing, sweet, wholesome harmony of a congregation joined purposefully together. And, I still do.

Easter sunrise service on the lawn, dew glistening in the breaking sun, majestic service of devotion, was a perfect place for seeing God's presence. I believe that it still is.

I used to think evidence of God's presence was in that stunning mountaintop, expansive ocean, fields of grain, flat distance of plains, in that creek bed, indescribable sunset, thunderous storm, budding flower, delicate spider web. And, I still do.

God's presence was exemplified in others, in goodness, in deeds and in service, in birth and in death, in ceremonies, funerals, processions. I believe that it is.

I saw God in connections with people and moments in time, coincidence, serendipity, miracles, recoveries, sacrifice, devotion, and love. I felt God's presence as that warm, secure feeling of belonging, knowing, sharing, discovering, joy, peace, love. And, I still do.

But, then, as I asked for God's help in getting out of our house when our neighborhood was on fire, the winds howling, the flames threatening, the embers hitting the house, my children asleep, the threat so great, I felt God so pronouncedly around me, such undeniable presence, a recognition of seeing God next to me, inside of me, around me like a fog is both present and untouchable, ethereal and markedly present. And, I knew that all the other times I saw God, I got a taste, through situations, feelings, emotions, people, nature, moments, messages, I had a taste, true and real, but a taste as small as a crumb at a banquet. A flicker of candlelight in the depths of night.

And, I was awed at the definitiveness, the pronounced evidence of God, God's presence, near and with me, available, reachable, accessible. The gravity, depth, breadth, magnitude of presence.

It made me wonder, can I experience God on that same level, that same pronounced depth without the traumatic circumstance, without stress. Can we see God, are we seeing God, are we missing out on seeing God all the time, in every moment, in all of the people around us, in every connection?

When Mother Teresa revealed in a recently published compilation of letters that during a period of many decades she never saw God, she did not feel the presence of God in her life, that she was disappointed that, in all her years of service, she never had the opportunity to see God; her comments really took me by surprise. She wrote, "I feel just that terrible pain of loss, of God not wanting me, of God not being God, of God not really existing." Mother Teresa was such an extraordinary person, having devoted her entire life to the service of others.

I wonder what her expectation was of how God's presence would be visible to her. Was she expecting a physical presence, a vision, a man, Caucasian, middle aged or elderly, with a white light shining from behind him or a halo over his head? What is "seeing God" supposed to look like, whether you are Mother Teresa or any other person?

The more I thought about it, the more perplexed I became. After all, Mother Teresa was exceptional, beyond compare, selfless, tireless. If she never saw God, or lost sight of God, then what is the likelihood any of the rest of us will experience seeing God? Perhaps she was being challenged in the way that Job was tested and held to his faith. Surely, she is the model of devotion and sacrifice, and she continued to serve throughout her years of conflict regarding her relationship with God.

I am a regular, ordinary person- mother, wife, attorney, community volunteer. Yet, I am confident that I have seen God- in the way that I believe God's presence is available to our eyes. I feel comfortable attesting to my witness of God near me, in me, around me. Not in physical, male form. Rather as energy in a form that was as a palpable as any presence, tangible, unmistakable, whole.

When we were trapped in the middle of the night in the San Diego wildfires, the threat profound, as merely specks of dust on the spectrum of human existence, small in our contribution, vulnerable in our lack of knowing, I prayed to God for help, over and over in my mind, desperate and pleading. And, I felt a presence of God around me, tangible and whole, and at the same time ethereal. Like fog or a rainbow. Undeniably present and yet impossible to grasp. A difficult description to comprehend and, yet, when I experienced it for myself, I understood completely all those descriptions I had heard before of God around us, near us, above and below us, inside each of us, light, presence, energy, love.

I believe we have the opportunity to see God much more that we realize, or exercise. This book is about those times when the presence of God was undeniable, God on earth, palpable, visible to my consciousness. The undefinable yet unmistakable awareness of God's presence is seeing God. And, when we see God, we are energized and loved and find purpose and meaning and feel the wholeness of the universe and find we are interconnected. Here are some of my personal experiences, spiritual messages and life lessons.

First, God's presence in defining moments of faith, during the wildfires, my pact with God as a child, a woman I met at nursing home, and my grandfather's gift in saying goodbye. Next, I include personal stories of hope in generosity and harsh lessons, through spiritual guides, angels, mentors, and friends. Then, after faith and hope, stories of God's presence in the spirit of love, spiritual messages and life lessons through the gifts and lessons of my children, husband, friendship, forgiveness, hardship.

I am early on this journey, puzzle pieces seemingly handed to me just one at a time, I struggle more often than not. My focus is to share a portion of my journey and inspire you as I have been inspired by the gifts I have received, knowing that I have much, much more to learn and that we are connected in this journey. For, as I put my heart out to you, you refill and fuel me.

And, you will find in reading, it is you that serves to inspire me. I am awed by the untapped potential of faith, hope, and love that is available to harness, collectively, humanitarianly, to bring us to a more spiritual realm. Because God is love. God is in each of us. Seeing God is seeing God in each of us, recognizing the love that is God's presence.

FAITH

FAITH- HOPE, TRUST, BELIEF.

ONCE, I TALKED TO A woman on a flight to San Diego, she was very nervous about flying, fumbling with her rosary beads. After the flight got off to a smooth start and she began to relax, I asked her about her nerves and about her faith. None of us know, she said. All of us are weak- just trying our best, but weak, nonetheless. So, how do we have a relationship, how to we move closer to God, to see him more clearly in our lives, I asked. Through prayer, she said. Pray. Pray all the time.

What do we pray, I asked.

Anything, she answered. Anything.

Just pray.

Are there defining moments with regard to faith? You either believe or you don't, right? If only it were that easy for us- sinners, sincere but human, driven to distraction, unsure how to approach feeling the presence of God,

1

not sure what it means when someone speaks of seeing God, not wanting to question, wanting to accept, but thinking the whole thing should be a little easier.

I think sometimes that our struggle with seeing God or feeling a need to see God is based on our looking at God like we look at Jesus, as we are taught as children in Sunday school. We see pictures of this great person, the son of God, and hear of all these great things that he did and stories from all these people in the bible that were privileged to witness his compassion, love, service, devotion, and we want to see God in that same way- physical form, performing great feats, nodding his approval at us, taking us by the hand or holding up his hand and pointing us in the right direction. Perhaps sunlight surrounding him, a huge strong presence, something very tangible.

Yet, we are blessed to see God every day in everything, all around us. Sometimes our eyes are open, our spirit still, really listening, and we ask, in prayer, for God's help.

And, when we ask, and when we listen, we really do see God.

Four stories of faith- the trauma of being in the middle of a wildfire and calling upon God's presence to guide us, my pact with God, a woman in a nursing home who helped me understand my contribution to her and her to me, and my grandfather who showed me life after death. God on Earth, present, available, near, accessible. And, the life lessons along the way.

Matthew 17:20 I tell you the truth, if you have faith as small as a mustard seed, you can say to this mountain, 'Move from here to there' and it will move. Nothing will be impossible for you.

THE FIRE

Revelation 3:20 Here I am! I stand at the door and knock. If anyone hears my voice and opens the door, I will come in and eat with that person, and they with me.

I OPENED OUR SOLID WOOD FRONT door to a seemingly endless expanse of red glowing sky menacingly searing through the velvet, pitch black night and I thought to myself- Oh my God, we are going to die.

How close have you been to death, my mind asked me. Reach out and touch it close, see it coming close?

Knowing the threat, looking and understanding with immediate recognition that I am no match for the fury of fire, heightened my awareness of the blood pulsing through my veins such that I could hear the rush as it moved past my ears and feel the pounding of each beat of my heart. A layer of cold sweat covered my back and legs, the small hairs on the nape of my neck and around my temples stood on end.

Everyone in the house was sound asleep except for me and Casey, my eleven year old son, who had begged that we evacuate hours earlier when we put him to bed. I felt the smoldering hot swirling wind on my bare arms and legs and the walls suddenly seemed paper-thin around me, my tennis shoes inadequate for the terrain or fire.

I could not go to sleep earlier that night. Maybe it was the promise to my son, Casey, that everything would be okay, that I was tracking the fire's progress, that someone would warn us to leave if need be. Maybe it was the fact that it was my birthday.

My birthday, a day of new beginnings, endings, symbolism, celebration, reflection and wildfires. It was my birthday and the skies were on fire in San Diego County. Still many miles from our home, I kept a watchful eye on the sky, radio on nearby, and enjoyed a markedly warm October day, with exceptional winds- hot, swirling Santa Ana winds.

I listened into the night, watched the news, even walked down the street several times, for hours kept vigil when unexpectedly Casey walked into my office and said he was unable to sleep because of the rain hitting his window. Rain? I laughed. It is not raining, silly. Come with me, to the living room, lay down by me on the living room couch. I will stay with you. Everything is okay.

I sat with him and thought of his fears, his sweet soul, and wondered how I could better reassure this child of mine who shouldered so much worry for all of us. Meantime, I kept thinking I should go to sleep too. After all, my seven year old would be awake by six o'clock in the morning and would be full of boundless energy. If I went to sleep now, I could squeeze in two and a half hours of sleep.

Matthew 5:8-9 Blessed are the pure in heart, for they will see God. Blessed are the peacemakers, for they will be called children of God.

No, I had reassured him, there was no need to evacuate, as the fires were a considerable distance away, we had not been alerted to leave, and I intended to stay up anyway, so I would make sure he was safe. We would leave, when and if, the time came.

Now, many hours later, I stood facing the blood red skies howling with the fury of fire as the Santa Ana winds whipped through the frenzied trees and debris flew through the air, much of it burning, and I thought of my son behind me.

Time slowed to fractions of seconds and was displayed before my eyes in frames, my senses on alert, every color more vivid, every sound deafening, more thoughts in succession than time would allow description, every word selected from brain to lips purposeful and direct.

Isaiah 41:13 For I am the LORD, your God, who takes hold of your right hand and says to you, Do not fear; I will help you.

It was my birthday. Synchrodestiny, no doubt.

In my head, I began to pray. Nothing complex; no poetry, no verse, no preparation- just a prayer, directly to God, to please, please help us. Please, Dear God, I begged, over and over again in my mind, just give us a couple of minutes, a couple of minutes to get out. That is all we need Lord. I can do the rest. Just a couple of minutes, please Dear God.

Suddenly, I was keenly aware of God's presence beside me, around me, near, present, close, tangible, whole. It was surprising and remarkable and, yet, somehow natural and expected, logical, my prayer realized as a presence accompanying me, surrounding me, about me.

Deuteronomy 4:29 But if from there you seek the LORD thy God, you will find him if you seek him with all your heart and with all your soul.

I turned to Casey and said, calmly and definitively, it is time to go, wake up Alec and get in the car. Then, I walked purposefully through our house to wake my husband.

We have four boys, one was at college and three were at home, a cat, a pet rat, husband and me. I counted as I prayed. Our youngest, age seven, is autistic. I would need to help him. I woke my husband. It is time to leave, I said. He looked quizzically at me and asked what was happening. No time, no time, I said. No time. Get everyone and get in the car.

Please Dear God, just a couple more minutes, just a couple more minutes, please God, I can do the rest. It was a mantra I chanted silently to myself, over and over again. I was feverishly begging in my mind as I spoke calmly to my children, as I counted the children in my mind.

And, the presence of God counted with me, silently, vividly, reminding me, accompanying me.

John 3:16 For God so loved the world, that he gave his only begotten Son, that whosoever believeth in him should not perish, but have everlasting life.

How abundant was my life that I had four children when others struggled to have any?

I could not help but count over and over again in my mind, each child, each pet, my husband, myself. Please dear God, is it too much to ask to spare us all?

Ephesians 3:14-21 For this reason I kneel before the Father, from whom his whole family in heaven and on earth derives its name. I pray that out of his glorious riches he may strengthen you with power through his Spirit in your inner being, so that Christ may dwell in your hearts through faith. And I pray that you, being rooted and established in love, may have power, together with all the saints, to grasp how wide and long and high and deep is the love of Christ, and to know this love that surpasses knowledge- that you may be filled to the measure of all of the fullness of God. Now to him who is able to do immeasurably more than all we ask or imagine, according to his power that is at work within us, to him be glory in the church and in Christ Jesus throughout all generations, forever and ever! Amen.

Entrusted with the care of so many, blessed with the responsibility, awed and overwhelmed with the duty of the moment, I prayed earnestly, counted deliberately, stepped forward decisively, each move weighty in its cumulative resultant impact, and wondered if it would be enough, fast enough, deliberate enough, admonishing myself not to panic, a steadfast focus on the objective at hand.

I woke Karrson, our 7 year old, and cheerfully told him that it was time to go, that he needed to go to the bathroom and get into the car. I helped him dress and walked him to the bathroom. Methodically, I put him in the minivan and strapped his seatbelt around him.

Please Dear God, just a couple more minutes.

Isaiah 40:29-31 He gives strength to the weary and increases the power of the weak. Even youths grow tired and weary, and young men stumble and fall; but those who hope in the LORD will renew their strength. They will soar on wings like eagles; they will run and not grow weary, they will walk and not be faint.

Karrson was a challenge from day one, though I could not put my finger on the challenge at hand. He simply exhausted me. He had boundless energy, and I attributed it to his desire to keep pace with his older three brothers. Karrson would cry at the slightest touch and then not cry from a serious fall. He would jump from the couch to the coffee table, couch to the coffee table, over and over again until he chipped his front tooth. Unfazed, he got right back up on the couch and started jumping again. He was ten months old.

He would climb onto the stove, and get into the tools in the garage. He would be fully dressed and swinging in the backyard one minute, then stark naked and carrying a shovel the next minute-digging a hole to China, and the earth's core is hot, hence sans clothing. I could not keep pace or anticipate his next move, or understand the chaotic mindset and extreme mood swings. When he was four, nearly five, he was diagnosed as autistic, which was more of an explanation than a solution. Karrson, named as Karen's son, is my heart; as sweet as sugar.

Zephaniah 3:17 The LORD your God is with you, he is mighty to save. He will take great delight in you, he will quiet you with his love, he will rejoice over you with singing.

When Karrson is the world's normal, he is a sheet of paper, utilitarian and resourceful, a love letter, scathing editorial, invitation, performance evaluation, Walt Whitman Americana. When Karrson is *his* normal, he is fireworks cascading like a waterfall or clamoring in a burst like waves crashing against a rocky shoreline, loud, fleeting, fiery and brilliant, disrupting the smooth velvety dark night sky, anticipated and unique. Thank you, God, for my barometer of the world around me.

I felt God with me, walking with me through the house, passing the walls filled children's artwork I had framed.

Joshua 1:9 Have I not commanded you? Be strong and courageous. Do not be afraid; do not be discouraged, for the LORD your God with be with you wherever you go.

Karrson was such an incredible artist. I had just framed his crayon drawing he titled "Birth" and put it on the living room wall. It showed a mother with a heart-shaped body and a baby with the umbilical cord from the belly button of child and mom connected, in the middle of the heart.

There was a salamander and a chicken. It was beautiful. Everything was vivid and smiling. I wanted that picture. I really, really wanted that picture. No time, no time. I know Lord, I know Lord. Thank you, Lord. Just a couple more minutes, please Lord. I can do the rest. If you can give me just a couple more minutes, Lord, I can do the rest.

I passed the pictures of the kids together, posed at the holidays, each wearing white and navy blue. They were bright eyed and beaming, young, sweet, innocent. In my mind, a thousand thoughts stuffed into each frame of time, I thanked the house, the walls, the roof, the floor that had protected us so well from the elements, a safe haven, a respite from the world, a desired place to sleep and recharge. I did not really want any one thing- I wanted the walls. I wanted it all. I wanted to wrap my arms around the walls and take it all with me. All that a house is, all that you want and create for yourself and your children. That is what I wanted to take with me. Thank you house, thank you God.

Jeremiah 17:7-8 But blessed is the man who trusts in the LORD whose confidence is in him. He will be like a tree planted by the water that sends out its roots by the stream. It does not fear when heat comes; its leaves are always green. It has no worries in a year of drought and never fails to bear fruit.

Time slowed even more as I moved swiftly and deliberately. I was consciously aware of frames of time, broken pieces of time, each moment solid and visible, concrete and fluid. It was as if I was now having millions of thoughts in just a second of time. Each precious second so full and vibrant, a story unfolding, a fluid dance of each of us moving together, interrelated but not touching, separate but not distinct, at once both dependent and autonomous.

The baby books, pictures of my grandfather who died when I was 14, the handmade Barbie doll clothing painstakingly made by my grandmother, the cherry cradle handmade by Mike's father where each child spent their first few months of life, our baby books, the handprint and footprint of kiln-fired clay framed and displayed, the stack of handmade mother's day cards all tied with a satin ribbon in my top dresser drawer, the Lionel train passed down from Mike's grandfather to father to Mike, the Christmas tree ornaments, the pictures of the kids, our wedding and honeymoon pictures, diaries, journal, books of poetry, my piano compositions, my short stories.

Memories flooding forward, washed into the present, potential laid out on display, what has been, what could be, this moment, stories woven together, no distinction, all time. No time, no time.

Just a couple of minutes, Lord. To escape the fire, Dear God- our family, our pets. Please Dear Lord.

Isaiah 43:18-19 Forget the former things; do not dwell on the past. See, I am doing a new thing! Now it springs up; do you not perceive it? I am making a way in the wilderness and streams in the wasteland.

Rebirth,
shedding of layers of the past,
burning of kah,
release from holding to the past
too strongly

The wildfires started on my birthday, Sunday October 21, 2007.

The night before, late in the evening Saturday night, my son Eric called. He was attending college at Southern Utah University in Cedar City. His voice was shaking as he explained he had taken a weekend road trip and was driving through the mountains from Denver back to school in Cedar City. He had hit a blizzard in his little Toyota Echo, he had just watched a semi go over the embankment in front of him, and he was panicked. He wanted to pull his car off the road and wait out the storm. He told me he was so tired, too tired to continue.

But, I knew how small his car was, how tiny the wheels, he had no coat, no hat, no water, no supplies, and if he stopped he could be hit by another car or not be able to start his car again and freeze out in the desolate mountain roads. I could not believe that he had even embarked on the trip, unbeknownst to us, with so little preparation and so little understanding of the elements and the circumstances.

I grew up in Michigan, Mike grew up in Wisconsin, but Eric had lived in San Diego since we moved to California when he was five years old. Now he was getting a crash course in driving in snow, he could barely control the car, and he was scared and exhausted. I knew exactly how serious the situation was and could hardly conceal my sheer terror that I was sitting in San Diego while he was on a curvy mountain highway, late at night, in a blizzard. I had him tell me the road markers as he passed each one, just in case the signal was lost and I had to report him missing to the state troopers.

It was nearly midnight as he drove and the fear in his voice was heartbreaking. I told him as gently as I could; please do not die on my birthday. Please Dear God, not on my birthday, please does not let him die on my birthday, I prayed. I kept him on the phone and coaxed him several miles to a hotel just off the next exit, called the hotel and gave them my credit card information and asked them to help him get chains and supplies for the trip home the next day.

Eric was born when I was just twenty four years old. He changed everything. My perspective, my objective, my self assessment, the resume and certificates of accomplishment obliterated in one fell swoop. I remember holding him when he was just three weeks old and thinking to myself- this, this is the most important thing I have ever done.

Eric, my firstborn- sweet, conscientious, always well-intended, truly absent-minded professor. Thank you, God. We were connected across those many miles, him in a blizzard, me about to be in a firestorm, and he reached for me, and I talked him through it, witness as much as if I were physically there. Thank you, God for continually showing me that being a mom is more important than anything I have ever done before in my life.

Romans 8:28 And we know that in all things God works for the good of those who love Him, who have been called according to His purpose.

That same night that Eric was driving through a blizzard with no coat, in a tiny ill-equipped car, my husband and another son, Alec, were camping with his Boy Scout troop on the Colorado River. On Sunday morning the temperatures were uncharacteristically hot and the winds were noticeably strong. Our patio chairs and umbrellas kept blowing around the backyard and I struggled to gather them and fold them. It was late October and we were going to celebrate my birthday that evening when Alec and Mike returned home around dinnertime. Casey and Karrson played together all morning and that afternoon Casey went with a friend to get pumpkins for Halloween.

It was so hot that we were all wearing shorts and enjoying the weather though the winds were strikingly strong at times. We heard on the radio about wildfires in Ramona and I knew that Mike would take one of two routes home from the campsite, one of which would take them dangerously close to the wildfires. I called and cautioned him about the fires and told him to alert the other fathers. They decided to take the longer, safer route home.

It was nothing short of a miracle that our second son, our fifteen year old, Alec, was able to participate in Boy Scouts.

I Peter 5:6-7 Humble yourselves, therefore, under God's mighty hand, that he may lift you up in due time. Cast all your anxiety on him because he cares for you.

When Alec was born, I asked my husband and the doctors what was wrong with his head. There was a ridge of bone with bumps running from his forehead to the crown of his head. Everyone assured me that Alec was fine, and that any abnormal appearance was due to the fact that he was born four weeks early. Alec did look unusual, with no eyebrows, no eyelashes, prominent eyes, and an underdeveloped jaw. These features I felt were attributable to his early birth, but his head, I knew something was wrong with his head.

Alec did not sleep for more than two hours at a time, screaming for hours upon waking and throughout the day. He would not nurse. And, over time his head became more and more misshapen. Alec preferred not to be held. I proceeded to take my newborn baby Alec, along with then three-year-old Eric, to numerous doctors to address the screaming and the bumps on his head.

Doctor after doctor condescendingly dismissed my concerns, telling me I was wrong, Alec's head was normal, there was nothing wrong with

Alec, I was overanxious, and I simply needed more rest or to take a pill for my unwarranted anxiety. The doctors assured me that he had colic, which he would outgrow. One doctor had the audacity to suggest after reflecting on Eric's blonde hair and blue eyes, that not every baby is a "Gerber" baby. Another doctor informed me that the reason my three-week-old baby did not want to be held was because he was independent.

Eight weeks and eight doctors later, I began to feel desperate.

Luke 12:48 But the one who does not know and does things deserving punishment will be beaten with few blows. From everyone who has been given much, much will be demanded, and from the one who has been entrusted with much, much more will be asked.

I called the Chief of Pediatrics at Riley Children's Hospital in Indianapolis where we lived. In order to get an immediate appointment, I lied to the receptionist, stating that I had been referred by his former colleague, an esteemed doctor and researcher at a prominent hospital in New York, and that his colleague said I needed to be seen immediately. She scheduled my appointment for just two days later. The first question the doctor asked me when I walked into his office with Alec was how I happened to know his former colleague. I told him that I did not know him; I confessed that I had lied in order to see him more quickly. This elder statesman doctor looked at me with kindness and a knowing recognition and remarked that I must be really desperate. Yes, I told him, holding back tears, yes, please help me, please fix my baby.

He diagnosed Alec with craniosynostosis and sent him on to neurosurgery but first explained that at just nine weeks old, Alec's head was completely fused. His brain was unable to grow. He needed to have a large portion of his skull removed to allow his brain to grow. The bone would grow back over time. He said he could not make promises about his recovery but, fortunately, we had arrived at his office in time. Had we arrived just four weeks later, he felt Alec's situation would be hopeless. Alec would never walk or talk; he would be permanently brain damaged with no hope of recovery. He could not make any promises but they would do everything they could to help him; we were there with no time to spare.

Four weeks. After just giving birth, three year old in tow, we had sought help from nine doctors in nine weeks, and found our answer only by the grace of a window of four weeks. God's gift to me. Alec was born four weeks early.

Alec, my second child- now healthy, whole, capable, and engaged. Thank you, God.

We fought for him, for weeks initially and then for years, fighting health insurance rejections, paying medical bills we could not afford, advocating for better and different treatments and eventually reaching firm ground, four brain surgeries later, an independent child, able to make his own way.

Thank you, God for incredible doctors and medical care. Thank you, God for giving me the determination to fight for Alec's medical care and showing me that I should trust my instincts and the guidance you have given me even in the face of criticism. And, that I have it within me to challenge and advocate on his behalf and for all of my children's needs.

Isaiah 55:11 ..so is my word that goes out from my mouth: It will not return to me empty, but will accomplish what I desire and achieve the purpose for which I sent it.

When Mike and Alec arrived home from their camping trip, Mike relayed to me that they had very little sleep, as most often happens on enjoyable camping trips, particularly attempting to sleep on the hard ground, had a wonderful time and were quite exhausted. Yet, after opening my birthday presents, enjoying a nice dinner, sharing camping stories, and watching the news about the fires, Alec and Mike were too hyped up to sleep and elected to stay awake that night as well.

We packed some clothes for work, the kid's backpacks for school, and decided we would take both cars if we were evacuated so that we would both be able to get to work and school with the kids. We thought we might be inconvenienced for a day to two, and packed a couple of outfits accordingly. Alec threw in a guitar at the last minute, but otherwise we had packed only those items that would carry us through a normal work week.

As the evening progressed, fatigue of camping set in, excitement waned, and they both went to sleep at one thirty in the morning. It was now about three forty, just two hours later, and while technically they were both awake, they were clearly out of it. Mike was operating on autopilot, getting dressed, car keys, wallet, sluggishly moving through rote motions. But, after Casey woke him, Alec did not come upstairs to the car. I went downstairs to find him, all the while conscious of the blessing that we still had electricity but might lose it at any time. What if I had to get everyone out without lights, I thought, as I wound through the downstairs hallway to his bedroom.

Alec was scooping bedding for his rat into a plastic container, scooping a small scoopful, over and over again. I did not want him to panic but I needed him to hurry. I sat down next to him, waited briefly, conscious of the time, the minutes, and then I told him that I really did not want to die in this house, we need to get out of here, now. He looked blankly at me, put his rat in the container and walked upstairs.

My heart was racing. So much time, so much time. I had asked God for minutes. How many was I being granted? Could I manage the rest?

How much time had passed since I opened the front door and looked at the raging skies, what was on fire, could we even get our cars out of the garage? Would we have to run through our neighborhood to safety? Carrying children in our arms? I thought again of my bare skin, shorts and tennis shoes.

Please Dear God, thank you God, thank you God, just a few more minutes, please I beg of you. Please, a few more minutes to get my family out safely. Please Dear God. I can do the rest.

A million thoughts, my mind moving so fast, my feet so slow and deliberate, trying to hurry, to not panic, each frame, each moment, an eternity. God present, around me, walking with me. Was it God's plan that we survive or die; what did God want from me to make this happen, to realize the safety of my family, to rescue us from fire.

I had not only decided to stay up all night; I had this sense that I should not go to sleep. Plus, I had promised Casey that I would make sure he was safe. And, yet, after everyone was asleep and it was just me, alone in the night, watching the news, reading the internet for news of the fire, listening to the radio, trying to find a source of information, I was not sure of my role. Nothing indicated I should stay awake or evacuate. There was no warning of danger or sirens, no flames in the distance, no smell of smoke.

News of the Witch Creek fire, located many miles away in Ramona, gave no indication of an immediate threat to our San Diego neighborhood. Little did anyone know, soon another fire, and there were many wildfires across Southern California at that point, the Guejito fire, would start in the San Pasqual Valley a few miles from our home, merge with the Witch Creek fire, winds would pick up in the Valley to nearly one hundred miles per hour, and firefighters would literally be forced to chase the fire as it raced throughout many San Diego County communities.

I walked outside several times, once down the middle of the street, looking, searching the skies for a sign that we should go. I did not want to wake my kids, unnecessarily scare them, disrupt my autistic son's routine, so critical to his well-being. And, so I stayed up, alone, waiting and watching but saw nothing, time and again. The neighborhood was completely still, quiet. The winds were warm and strong but nothing particularly ominous.

In fact, the neighborhood was eerily quiet, dark- everyone asleep or vacated? Were we the last to go or was everyone nestled comfortably in their beds, oblivious to the worry I was experiencing?

God is always with us,
Presence of Spirit,
Universal energy

Where was the signal that I should go? The assurance that I should stay?

Matthew 7:7 Ask and it will be given to you; seek and you will find; knock and the door will be opened to you.

Around two o'clock in the morning I felt foolish; staying awake, knowing that my youngest would wake at six o'clock, as he always does, full of energy and anticipation of the day ahead. I was wasting that precious sleeping time. I said to God, as I sometimes do, God what should I do- if I should leave, please give me a sign.

I am great at asking God all sorts of things, but terrible at listening to God's response. Because, in that moment, I was in our laundry room and the chimes just outside the window, by our magnolia tree and birdbath, chimes that are actually called Amazing Grace when you order them in the mail order catalog, mind you, rang violently loud. So loud, so abrupt, so startling that I ran to the bathroom, queasy in response, then scolded myself for being so silly and spooking myself.

Oh, yes, God answers your questions, your prayers, your thoughts, but how often are you listening? Do you really want to hear the answer? I was such a great question asker but not such a great answer listener.

Exodus 4:8-9 "Then it will be, if they do not believe you, nor heed the message of the first sign, that they may believe the message of the latter sign. And it shall be, if they do not believe even these two signs, or listen to your voice, that you shall take water from the river and pour it on the dry land. And the water which you take from the river will become blood on the dry land."

Now, I lamented my unwillingly to listen, to really hear, nearly two hours later, knowing, knowing the answer, confirmation of the sign, recognizing my failure to heed God's answer earlier in the night. And, afraid that it was too late.

The children were in the minivan, seatbelts on, the rat on Alec's lap, the cat under the seat in my car- how many kids, how many pets? Are we all here? We need to go, we need to go. The fire was visible through the small windows on the garage drawers. All the lights were still on in the house. I had my keys, my cell phone. Mike seated in the minivan, me in my smaller car.

When we opened the garage, debris blew into the garage, the wind howled, and the house seemed to strain against the powerful winds and the furor of the fire. Trees were on fire, a wall of flames was approaching, lapping forward like a huge red-orange wave slicing through the black sky, winds swirled burning branches on the ground and into the air, our three pepper trees in front of our house were catching much of the burning debris, sheltering us briefly between the fire and our house, granting us space and minutes, precious time.

And, all this time, Casey had been waiting in the car for the rest of us, watching the sky, seeing the flames obscure the black from the sky. Casey, our son who had wanted so desperately to leave early in the evening the night before. My gentle giant even as a toddler, Casey would help me unload the groceries, carrying a gallon of milk in each hand, when he was just two years old. He would worry about himself and everyone around him- is your seatbelt fastened, is your door locked, which diseases are contagious, watch out for that car ahead.

Now we would have to drive through the fires Casey had feared were coming to burn down our house. What will I say to him going forward when he presents another worry to me?

My gentle giant seemed so tiny and vulnerable sitting in his seat in the minivan. Everything seemed small framed against the wall of flames.

We need God even when we think we don't,
Our interdependence and relationship with the
Universal energy around us

Just a few minutes, please Lord.. I can do the rest..?

2 Corinthians 3:5 Not that we are competent in ourselves to claim anything for ourselves, but our competence comes from God.

I backed out of the garage, into the firestorm, out of the seeming safety, into the flames, later learning from a neighbor that a corner of our house was already on fire. Burning embers pelted the car making a loud thumping noise. I feared the car would catch fire, or stall, or be incapacitated if I ran over anything too big, too sharp. I marveled at the prospect of this shell being all that kept my bare skin, in shorts, short-sleeved top and tennis shoes, from burning.

Thank you, God for helping us escape, for getting us out of our house safely, together.

As a million thoughts raced through my head, still operating in still frames of time, slowed to such a degree that I could relay every thought and draw each picture but never be able to capture all and finish in my lifetime, I moved the car into drive and drove out of our semi-circular driveway and onto the dark, winding, narrow road. Fire illuminated the night, but otherwise, it was pitch black outside, a striking contrast of dark and light, the fire lapping at the houses and trees and us. It was moving as a wave, forward and back, then more forward and back again, reaching out for us to fuel it, feeding on the landscape. The smoke was so dense, the road was not discernible from the ditches and driveways lining each side. No sidewalks on our street, just a narrow two-laned road, curvy, tree-lined.

God is in that moment. God is all around us. The presence of God is palpable. Inside of you and outside of you. Present. In that moment.

Matthew 28:18-20 Then Jesus came to them and said, "All authority in heaven and on earth has been given to me. Therefore go and make disciples of all nations, baptizing them in the name of the Father and of the Son and of the Holy Spirit, and teaching them to obey everything I have commanded you. And surely I am with you always, to the very end of the age."

Mike was driving the minivan. I hated driving that car. It was too big, too high up, too hard for me to really see well. Now it sheltered everything, everything to me. He was behind me, following me. Or, so I thought.

I could not see to drive. Thank you, God, thank you for those minutes allowing us to get out of the house and to the safety of our car. But, now the smoke is so thick, the sky so black, the fire enveloping the street and houses, I cannot see to drive. The winds were extreme, my car shaking, debris bashing the car sides and rooftop. What am I thinking? I began to panic, the urgency of the situation overwhelming. And, it struck me what I had asked of God as I stood at the door, as I walked through the house, as I begged for our family's survival, for minutes, *I can do the rest.*

Who am I to say to God, please give me a minute, a few minutes, I can do the rest? I cannot do the rest. I need you, God. I need you to get me through all of this. I cannot see to drive. I don't know what to do and I need your help, God. I don't know why I would ask for minutes and expect to do the rest myself. I need you, God, for each and every step of this journey- not just today, but every day.

I just don't think about it, or ask for it, or appreciate that you are all around me, all the time, every day, every second, not just in moments of weakness but in every success, not just in terror, but also in joy. Please help me, God.

Proverbs 3:5-6 Trust in the LORD with all your heart and lean not on your own understanding; in all your ways submit to him, and he will make your paths straight.

A voice came in my head, as clear as pure as water. Karen, you have driven down this road a million times, a million times. Just close your eyes and drive. I nearly laughed at the prospect of driving with my eyes closed and, suddenly, I felt an extreme sense of peace and comfort. I know that in that moment I smiled. And breathed.

And, so I did. I closed my eyes and I listened to the bu-bump-bum as I drove. I listened and drove as fast as I could down our winding road, ditches and mature trees lining both sides, with my eyes closed. I cannot tell you truly what that felt like, to turn yourself completely over to God in that moment. But, I did.

2 Corinthians 5:7 We live by faith, not by sight.

Complete surrender, to the moment, to the circumstances, to God's direction. Trust, devotion, faith. Could you do it? I never would have imagined that would be me, driving with my eyes closed down a dark, windy road through a firestorm.

As the calm enveloped and carried me and I knew that I could do anything with God's help, I opened my eyes and glanced back in the rear view mirror for Mike, for the minivan. Nothing. I could see nothing.

Was that because of the thick smoke, the black sky, or was he just out of view? I called his cell phone. He did not answer. I stopped my car in the middle of the street.

Where was he? My heart was racing and panic grabbed at my throat. I was escaping the fire and my family was not? Did a tree fall and block his exit, did a child have to go to the bathroom just before he left and he was trapped inside our burning house?

We have the capacity of be present
- in the moment-
in a way that is profound
and attuned to all that is the
universe
that with the noise around us
is often difficult
to experience.

Should I turn around and go back?

Psalm 85:10-13 Lovingkindness and truth have met together; righteousness and peace have kissed each other. Truth springs from the earth, and righteousness looks down from heaven. Indeed, the LORD will give what is good, and our land will yield its produce. Righteousness will go before Him and will make His footsteps into a way.

Mike has always been the constant- reliable, unwavering, self assured, my foundation. We met in graduate school. I remember his broad, easy smile. Likeable, approachable, friendly. Mike had the highest SAT scores in the state of Wisconsin, was nominated to West Point, readily masters a subject, and easily dissects a test. I, on the other hand, had such low SAT test scores in English and high scores in Math that the Chair of the graduate program assumed that English was my second language. But, in our graduate program, I was first in our class and Mike was second. I still tease him about that now and then, knowing he is the more proficient in nearly everything.

There was a patrol car a short distance ahead. I drove forward, rolled down my window and he rolled down his. The winds raged and I shouted as loudly as I could to him – my husband, my children, they are behind me, they are not behind me, I don't know where they are, they need help, please help me. He looked back at me blankly, not able to discern my shouts over the thunderous sound of the fire. The smoke quickly filled my car- rancid, acidic, thick. I yelled back again, to no avail.

White flakes of ash covered me and the passenger seat. Embers, now bigger, now louder, still on fire, slammed against the roof and side of the car.

I called Mike again. He answered. I was relieved but still panicked at the thought that he was trapped.

Where are you, where are you?

I am driving, he said.

I cannot see you, where are you?

I am coming, he answered. I am driving slowly because I cannot see. I don't want to go off the road, he explained.

I am driving as fast as I can because I don't want to burn up in the fire, I said pleadingly.

Hurry, Hurry. How about if you drive faster and I drive slower and we can get out of this together, I suggested, holding back tears.

Yes, yes, I am coming, he answered.

I drove forward, thinking that the smoke was so thick, he could come upon my car and hit it before either of us realized the other was there. We both drove to the entrance of our neighborhood. Fire trucks passed us. At last, fire trucks. We drove to the highway.

James 4:10 Humble yourselves before the Lord, and he will lift you up.

Thank you, God, thank you. I said faster and faster to myself, over and over again. Thank you, God, thank you. Thank you, God, thank you. I called my husband again. No longer able to control myself, sobbing as I drove.

I was so afraid, so afraid, I told him. I cannot drive, I was so afraid.

You can, he told me. Follow me.

And, so, I followed him first to the animal hospital to drop off our pets and then downtown to a hotel. On the phone with him, crying and driving.

*Know
that your place
in the universe
at any given
moment
is any-where
and every-where*

2 Corinthians 9:8 And God is able to make all grace abound to you, so that in all things at all times, having all that you need, you will abound in every good work.

Our home burned down in the San Diego wildfires. It was traumatic, dramatic, and all the adjectives you can muster to describe it. We escaped barely, within minutes of our home being engulfed in flames, and we are grateful. Every second in those moments between seeing the red sky, realizing the imminent danger, backing toward flames two stories tall, embers rolling into our garage, the crunch of the burning debris as we drove away, the smoke so thick we could not see to drive, the rote memory we relied on that we knew each curve in the roads, the wave of fire lapping at our home, the smell, the sound, the fury, the deliberateness with which we placed each child in the car, the cat, the pet rat, the feeling in my gut that we would never return to this home, and the gratitude we felt toward this structure that had nestled us safely for five years, the glance I gave to each room as I swiftly walked by, memorizing and knowing there was nothing and everything that I wanted to grab and take and knowing there was no minute, not even a second, to spare to even consider such frivolity.

Yes, I am grateful. If you know me at all, you know that I am. Truly. Blessed.

I begged God to give us just a minute more to escape safely, just a few minutes, promising that I could do the rest, that I had the resources to make it if He would grant just me a few minutes more.

And, the recognition that I cannot do the rest, not alone anyway.

And, I want you to know that once we reached a main road and made our way to the highway, I spent every second I had saying thank you. Yes, gratitude. My pain is deep, don't miss that message. You cannot feel pain without first having experienced great joy. And, the protection, safety, and memories of that home gave us great joy. God helped us every step of the way. God is all around us, in us, near us, next to us, present, visible, physical, spiritual, available, accessible. I am grateful for having and seeing God's presence around me as we escaped the fire.

Psalm 50:23 He who sacrifices thank offerings honors me, and he prepares the way so that I may show him the salvation of God.

The fire touched everyone. So many people were significantly impacted. There were numerous fires all burning at the same time, throughout southern California. In San Diego County alone, over five hundred thousand people were evacuated, nearly four hundred thousand acres of land burned, more than fifteen hundred homes were destroyed, many more homes were damaged, there were numerous injuries including firefighters, and people lost their lives trying to escape, trapped in the fires.

When I talk about the fire, I get lost in my head because it was so overwhelming and so, when people ask about what I took away from the fire (sort of a lesson learned), I often do not really answer the question very directly – mostly because there is so much to consider.

But, in fairness, what did you learn from the wildfire, is a fair question and deserving of an answer- it is just there is no simple answer. To mention a few things:

1. Rebirth, shedding of layers of the past, burning of kah, release from holding to the past too strongly;
2. God is always with us, presence of Spirit, Universal energy;
3. We need God even when we think we don't, our interdependence and relationship with the universal energy around us;
4. We have the capacity to be present- in the moment- in a way that is profound and attuned to all that is the universe that with the noise around us is often difficult to experience; and
5. Knowing your place in the universe at any given moment is any-where and every-where.

Colossians 3:15-17 *Let the peace of Christ rule in your hearts, since as members of one body you were called to peace. And be thankful. Let the message of Christ dwell among you richly as you teach and admonish one another with all wisdom through psalms, hymns, and songs from the Spirit, singing to God with gratitude in your hearts. And whatever you do, whether in word or deed, do it all in the name of the Lord Jesus, giving thanks to God the Father through him.*

Puppy Love and Promises

1 John 5:14-15 This is the confidence we have in approaching God: That if we ask anything according to his will, he hears us. And if we know that he hears us- whatever we ask- we know that we have what we asked of him.

MY FASCINATION WITH ANIMALS, WILDLIFE, birds, plants, gardening, rocks, trees, and nature began when I was very young. To my mother's dismay, my lack of fear and fondness for snakes and other reptiles meant many terrifying surprises for her as I felt compelled to share my newfound treasures, usually popping into the kitchen as she was washing dishes, me proudly carrying some, in her words, slimy, threatening creature.

Shoeboxes became incubators for caterpillars. Potato bugs dominated the underside of rocks around our willow tree. Nests returned to branches, lost cats returned to owners. I loved watching birds, chasing butterflies, even staring for hours at a praying mantis on a branch outside the window.

I would try to befriend rabbits, squirrels and chipmunks, but even those gave my mother pause, and, once, an errant chipmunk that wandered into our house created a ruckus, resulting in my broom-armed mother standing on a chair while our neighbor, an elderly gentleman who wandered over to survey the commotion chuckled loudly and propped open a door to allow the relieved little creature to escape.

Trees were for climbing and tree houses or swinging on branches. I collected all different species of leaves and classes of rocks and set out to identify insects, birds, moths, butterflies, even worms, though they were not collected. I would sneak a few specimens in the house for a time, buried in a cup of dirt, but my excitement and our single bathroom home, where all collected items were rinsed, gave me away. I managed to have some pet fish and ant farms. A pet turtle, Mr. Red Eye, met his untimely death after crawling into my mother's shoe. But, most of my joy for animals was experienced by exploring outdoors, reading, television programs, field trips to the zoo, and visiting our neighbors' pets.

Two puppies lived across the street from our house, kept in a small wire cage in a garage. Sisters, named for the lakes that bordered the campgrounds where they were born, Kimball and Pickerel. Pickerel was fearless and feisty and would take off at the slightest opportunity, running fast and furious, eyes buried beneath some of the thick, curly black and white hair that covered her. Unapologetic in her fury to escape the confines of the small wire enclosure on the cold cement garage floor, single water bowl, single empty food bowl. Michigan winters are harsh. Kimball, nearly all black with just a diamond of white fur on her chest, was much more shy and cooperative, waiting approval and acknowledgement before stepping outside the boundaries of her cage. Her hair was curly but not wild curly like Pickerel, the hair reflecting in part, the personalities.

When the owner went out of town, I took care of the puppies. Pickerel would take off as fast as she could and I would panic, calling and chasing and calling some more. She thought it was a great game, me chasing, her running, but, as an eight year old, saddled with responsibility for her care, I did not relish her joy. I loved Kimball. She was sweet and timid and I felt bad that her spirit was not undeterred like Pickerel's admirable, brave soul.

Our family purchased a puppy, Waddles, named for her gait and, perhaps, the consistently full bladder that accompanied the shuffle. Nearly as soon as she arrived at our house, Waddles ate a large hole in our family room couch and, thus, was promptly returned from whence she came. I was so surprised by the turn of events. There, then gone. Promptly. No discussion, no vote, no democracy. The dog ate a hole in the couch, the end. Not unreasonable, I suppose. Just shocking.

And, thus the stage was set for a beginning to my formal relationship with God…

Proverbs 20:11 Even a child is known by his actions, by whether his conduct is pure and right.

We attended church fairly regularly, and I participated in Sunday school and choir.

I believed in God.

But, from the mind and heart of an innocent child, mine, when my newly acquired dog was abruptly removed from our home and I watched the two dogs across the street, one a free spirit and one becoming beaten down, I recognized an obvious injustice and inequity that plagued me.

Earnestly, I prayed to God.

Dear God. Please give me a dog – either the dog across the street, Kimball, or a dog just like her, one black with a little diamond of white on her chest. I would add a lengthy physical description and description of Kimball's personality. At the end, every time, I concluded- If you do, Dear Lord, I will believe in you forever. Please, please dear God.

Matthew 18: 4-6 Therefore, whoever humbles himself like this child is the greatest in the kingdom of heaven.

Now, you and I, as adults know that you are not supposed to test God. But, when you are eight years old and making a pact with God, right or wrong, it is serious business. And, so I set forth with the business of praying. And, I prayed diligently for many weeks, daily, nightly, with all my heart and soul.

One day, my parents sat me down in the living room with a graveness typically reserved for serious proceedings such as a funeral procession. They announced solemnly- we are going to be getting a dog, the dog across the street, Kimball. Yes, I beamed. Yes, I know, I know, I answered to their confused glances at each other. Because I prayed for her, every single day, day and night, for many, many days. I asked for her. And, we are getting her. God answers prayers, if you really believe.

And, from that day, *and all the days before,* I have honored my agreement- to believe in God forever.

I was a child, a believer of God, who challenged God but with the purest of intent, to save that dog and to have the opportunity to love her like she should be loved. I know in my heart that my motives were pure and that I just wanted that dog more than anything. In my childish mind, my devotion the only bargaining chip I thought I had to use. Ironically, my test of abandoning God meant relying on God for assistance. My many prayers to God an acknowledgement of my faith, my belief that God would answer.

James 5:16-18 Therefore confess your sins to each other and pray for each other so that you may be healed. The prayer of a righteous person is powerful and effective. Elijah was a human being, even as we are. He prayed earnestly that it would not rain, and it did not rain on the land for three and a half years. Again he prayed, and the heavens gave rain, and the earth produced its crops.

Kimball proved an excellent companion, great listener, ready playmate. She would bound through the Michigan knee-deep snow like a bunny hopping in and out of depressions or making her own, readily dive into a freshly raked pile of leaves, and quickly race to place herself squarely in the middle of the frame any time a camera was in sight. She never begged for food except for chocolate, her favorite chocolate ice cream, a treat on a hot, humid Michigan summer day.

As kids, when we were charged with finishing our lunch before returning outside to play, we would feed her under the table, whatever vegetables we did not like. Kimball often did not like them either, so we would get in trouble when a pile of peas were housed between table leg and our own. But, she would munch happily on potato chips and we would cough loudly to try to mask her chomping.

She ran toward the refuge of the back door when a mink made its way into our yard, until we happened outside and then she bee-lined for the intruder, ever dutiful in her role as protector, the stench unbearable. Always fearful of men, she would give a low growl when a man entered the yard but would readily make friends if he presented as friendly.

Of course, a lot has happened since I was eight years old and a lot has happened to solidify my belief in God, to teach me that one does not test God in order to prove God does exist, and to show me that God was always present, before, after, and during the whole dog ordeal.

As an adult, my belief in God, while constant, wanders and wanes at times, I lose focus, and when I am called upon, I go to those moments of prayer to God as a child wherein I threw all my heart and soul into steadfast prayer with the unreserved belief that my prayers would be answered. Today, I still believe that God answers every single prayer, I just also know that praying for the winning lottery ticket is not an honest use of my faith. And, a lack of honest prayer will result in what I need, much more than what I think I want.

Romans 12:12 Be joyful in hope, patient in affliction, faithful in prayer.

Isn't a child-life belief in God, full of wonder, anything is possible, unreserved, all in, base, elemental, raw, really the goal? Much as we like to complicate God, the bible, and the symbols, signs, events in our lives to make something manifest with the profoundness worthy of a label of miracles, the most simplistic of measures is the more profound evidentiary moment of God in our lives.

Does it have to be an explosion, lighting, fire, when the reality is the faintest of moments, the first breath of life, no more profound than any other, largely the pinnacle one of import? That slight gasp, that whisper of presence, the tingle up your spine when someone is standing directly behind you, with not a sound, but you sense the closeness, the most basic of a glance and suddenly seeing, a touch and finally feeling.

I loved that dog so much and she loved me. I had never felt so deeply such unconditional love. That is a dog, for you. They greet you warmly, so matter how long you have been gone. No scolding for the lengthy abandon, just sheer joy that you have returned. They will accompany you anywhere, up for any game, activity, or just a nice scratch on the belly or ear. Dogs don't care what you make for dinner- hamburger or steak- although they prefer either over dog food. They could care less about how you look, smell, if you track in mud on your shoes, if you can't find the right words, if you aren't the fastest runner or top student in the class.

Dogs just embrace a commitment that they are yours, with complete, steadfast, permanent, forever devotion. They want to be always by your side. Dogs want any opportunity they can get to show you just how much you are loved.

Made all the more special that she was a gift from God. One gift actually, a small gift among many, though seemingly a huge gift to me at the time, one small pebble skipped across a horizon into a pond of endless, bottomless, breadth of God's boundless gifts. Thank you God for illustration of devotion and demonstrable unconditional love, a gift to a child, so that in my child's mind I would see and understand a tiny example what devotion looks like and how vast unconditional love can present.

Have I ever committed myself that fully to any other relationship?

How deep is my devotion-deep like a dog loves his master, deep like the gifts that God grants me readily each and every day, whisper it quietly with uncertainty deep or stand up and shout it out loud deep?

A commitment to believe forever- yes. Steadfast devotion, accomplished by child-like devotion, as from child-worthy belief.

God forgives and accepts our child-like devotion.
Any glimpse of unconditional love we have experienced pales in comparison to God's unconditional love for us.
Our challenge is to retain an unadulterated belief in God.

Unconditional love. Steadfast devotion. Pure belief, magical, possible, all in.

Lesson learned. Impression made.

Forever.

Psalm 71:5 For you have been my hope, Sovereign LORD, my confidence since my youth.

Romans 8:38-39 For I am convinced that neither death nor life, neither angels nor demons, neither the present nor the future, nor any powers, neither height nor depth, nor anything else in all creation, will be able to separate us from the love of God that is in Christ Jesus our Lord.

MRS. BEARD

Romans 12:3-8 For by the grace given me I say to every one of you: Do not think of yourself more highly than you ought, but rather think of yourself with sober judgment, in accordance with the faith God has distributed to each of you. For just as each of us has one body with many members, and these members do not all have the same function, so in Christ we, though many, form one body, and each members belongs to all the others. We have different gifts, according to the grace given to each of us. If your gift is prophesying, then prophesy in accordance with your faith; if it is serving, then serve; if it is teaching, then teach; if it is to encourage, then give encouragement; if it is giving, then give generously; if it is to lead, do it diligently; if it is to show mercy, do it cheerfully.

HER NAME WAS MRS. BEARD. And, yes, she had one. Long dark wiry hairs planted firmly on her thin, pale translucent skin. A large wispy fluff of very white hair plopped haphazardly on her head. Her long, thin fingers grabbed at my arm or hand, a firm strong grip, crippled in odd configurations with arthritis. She would lean in close to tell me something dramatic, her breath stale, her teeth rotted, her eyes fiery and dancing playfully amongst her jagged features. A petite build, quick gait, razor sharp mind, pleasant demeanor, thoughtful words strung together and released poignantly from her tongue.

1 Thessalonians 1:3 We continually remember before our God and Father your work produced by faith, your labor prompted by love, and your endurance inspired by hope in our Lord Jesus Christ.

She had been an organist for her church and told tales of her days there. A wistful faraway haze consumed her face as she spoke, mellowing her hard lines, softening her voice to nearly a whisper. She spoke fondly of her prior ability to play the piano and organ, her prominent role in the church, her inability to fully uncurl her knuckles locked into disjointed angles across her hand. She brushed her long bangs from her hair into the fluff of hair with the back of her hand and would tug at her skirt to ensure its proper length. She was quick on her feet and would jump up to see me, quick to embrace me and lean in for a secret exchange of ideas, a whisper shared between friends.

My job at age fourteen was to talk to the nursing home residents. To brighten their day. I was a "Pleasanteer" charged with being "pleasant" and engaging to anyone that cared to spend time with me.

The facility was stuffed brim full of people needing cheering. I would walk the sterile, wide halls and peer into a dark room to see a small figure on a large recliner or rocking chair, pressed close to the window with blinds drawn tight, barely discernible in the sliver of light, a dark, lonely shadow of a former independent soul.

Once I discovered an elderly woman sitting in a large bathtub, naked, with just a few inches of water covering her cold, bare body. She was forgotten, having spent the night adrift in the deep porcelain vessel.

I would peer into a room and hesitate, reluctant to intrude on the small semblance of privacy remaining to a resident but wanting to avail myself to those present. I feared walking by as another rejection, more confirmation of abandonment. And, so, I would steady myself and cheerily smile and loudly call out a greeting and see what kind of response I might receive.

More often than not, I left the nursing home gulping large volumes of fresh air, bounding down the cement stairs, rushing home, fearing turning my head back lest someone cast a forlorn look in my direction. I cried a lot. Am I helping, Lord? And, I returned and returned and returned. Sometimes I would ask myself how I could do it- to return. And, more often than not, I would ask myself, how could I not.

Mrs. Beard was special. An articulate shiny pearl in the murky sea of sadness, beaming endlessly at me at soon as she lit upon the tapping of my shoes announcing my arrival down the hallway.

Sometimes a group would gather and I would organize a game or activity. Other times, I would just visit with someone and hear tales of children and grandchildren, spouses lost to war, years gone by, stories told as if the event occurred the day before. Storytellers so lost in the story that they would lose a sense of who I was and why I was there, asking me if a son or daughter was soon to arrive. I never knew how to address those questions of why and where and when are they coming to visit. I did not even know if they lived nearby for a visit to be imminent or possible.

It was a helpless and fulfilling role that I played. So inadequate, incompetent, a poor substitute for a husband, daughter, grandchild. A drop of water to a desert of famine stricken people. Other times, I felt I gave presence and attention and love in a vast void, but wondered if that void could be penetrated, so deep and cavernous a wound I could not discern if the attention was lost or captured. Water dripping into a deep sun baked clay pot. A storyteller so lost in a story that time would pass and the room so dark and my presence so still, did he or she even remember that I was there. As time would pass and a voice would weaken or rise and fall, I would have to slip quietly out to end my day or turn the patient over to a nurse for the next dose of medications.

And, so, one day, having felt so taxed and inadequate, and wholly incapable of understanding or appreciating any value to my role, wondering what, if any, benefit I played or rather if I was more a reminder that they were alone, I had a conversation with Mrs. Beard that led me down a path of enlightenment.

James 2:17-18 In the same way, faith by itself, if it is not accompanied by action, is dead. But someone will say, "You have faith; I have deeds." Show me your faith without deeds, and I will show you my faith by my deeds.

We were talking about her role as pianist and organist, about her passion for music in general, about her frustration at no longer being able to play, and I, who was no pianist by any stretch of imagination but I could fumble through some basic piano music, took some of the worn pages of music that she held up before me and walked over to the upright, out of tune

35

piano, moved my hand across the dusty keys, balanced the music against the broken stand and jumped into my rendition of some yellowed pages of church music, all deep chords, repetitive, recognizable. I began playing more, bumbling through but with some commitment, and Mrs. Beard scurried over to join me on the bench.

She squeezed in tight, right next to me, our hips pressed together; she moved her hands over mine and moved them up and down in the air along with the music. I hesitated and then began to play louder and louder as she closed her eyes and sang, her hands never hesitating, her voice strong, unwavering. We played together, the same song many, many times and then a few more songs.

We have the capacity to serve, give, nurture, care for, love, attend to, honor, respect, provide, and assist someone in his or her desire to serve, any time, any place.

Our acts of service exemplify faith.

Tears streamed from her tightly shut eyes and her voice quivered at times but rang out the songs as she so aptly remembered them. Music, her act of service, demonstration of faith, gift to share. She knew God, she served her church and the people of her church, and longed to serve some more- with action and voice. She longed to serve, and lived in frustration at her inability to serve through her music, and my hands coupled with her desire and voice, her urging, guiding, encouraging me, I was able to assist her in service.

Our relationships serve as the conduit to service, as the nexus to God, as we give love as he has asked and as he has demonstrated to us.

I helped her and she helped me, to find myself, my role, my contribution in that seemingly empty, cold, cavernous despair. So much longing there, so much faith. She showed me a commitment to God and faith, an appreciation for the presence of God any and every where.

Mrs. Beard. Yep, she had one. An odd mix of crippled features, a worn figure housing a strong spirit. One of the most beautiful women I have ever met.

Ecclesiastes 4:9-12 Two are better than one, because they have a good return for their labor: If either of them falls down, one can help the other up. But pity anyone who falls and has no one to help them up. Also, if the two lie down together, they will keep warm. But how can one keep warm alone? Though one may be overpowered, two can defend themselves. A cord of three strands is not quickly broken.

Still Near

1 Chronicles 29:17 I know, my God, that you test the heart and are pleased with integrity. All these things I have given willingly and with honest intent. And now I have seen with joy how willingly your people who are here have given to you.

WHEN I REFLECT BACK ON who has had the most influence on me in my life, one of the people, probably at the top of that list, would be my grandfather, even though he died when I was only fourteen years old. Recently, I went to the funeral of my aunt, his daughter. At the viewing, I had the opportunity to talk to Richard, my grandfather's brother. I told him that I could not believe we were at a funeral for my aunt when I still miss my grandfather who died over thirty years ago.

I told him that his brother still remains one of the most influential people in my life. Richard gave a knowing smile and said that his own father died when Richard was just ten years old, eighty years prior. And, yes, he understood, how someone so long ago taken from your life could still hold such prominence. Richard and I both have a tie to his brother, my grandfather, from the events that occurred in the early morning hour of his death.

If you knew my grandfather, rock solid, tough, strong farmer that he was, you would never suspect that he would be the one to bring me evidence of angels and heaven, the permanence of light, our return to energy on another plane, a future, the afterlife. He did not speak about dying and heaven, or sugarcoat anything. My grandfather was pretty definitive with his words, straightforward, conventional.

He was definitely a believer in God and people, the bible, church, all the principles of religion, devotion, dedication, commitment and faith. So, maybe all the better, credible, and meaningful that it would be his message to me, the evidence he would provide, that would point to God's presence, demonstrable, visible, tangible.

My grandmother combed his hair every morning, a nice straight part accomplished after several deliberate attempts, just right, slicked down the cowlicks, several times, finally resorting to wetting her finger with her tongue, smoothing flat the stubborn hairs. Rosie he called her. Rosalyn. Nothing compared to the sound of him saying her name. It was different-Rosie- said from his lips than from anyone else. She would laugh, oh stop it, she would say, then laugh some more.

He was a farmer, then a security guard, took care of his family, his wife, children, grandchildren. My grandmother worked the farm alongside him, plowing the fields, canning fruit, feeding the men huge breakfasts of eggs and bacon.

The world stopped when we were near. Treated as prominent guests, to hearty meals, card games, and long conversations about our affairs as children, important matters of friends, school, conflicts with each other, questions of import about the world, politics, human behavior. My grandmother would lavish us with huge feasts of roast beef, ham, mashed potatoes, gravy, beans, carrots, rolls, slow baked all day long on low, pie and cake, ice cream and cookies too. We were indulged to our fill and beyond, never a sign of loss of interest, or trumped by matters of precedence.

She loved Johnny Cash and played *Ring of Fire* and we, the grandkids, would dance, on the circular rug in the basement, pretending we were dancing round a large fire in the center, round and round we would run and dance and sing loudly. Johnny Cash and Elvis. Blue Suede Shoes and ballads. We would watch Elvis movies too. Grandpa would fall asleep in his recliner chair and snore louder than the music or us laughing and when he would wake we would tell him stories of his snoring which he adamantly refused to believe.

I remember he referred to someone as Black and I corrected him by saying African American. He told me that when he was growing up, his best friend was Joe. Joe and my grandfather played baseball together, went to school together, shared the same friends, and had each other's back. First Joe was Negro, then he was Colored, then he was Black. Now, my grandfather sternly said to me, you are telling me that Joe is African American and all I know is that Joe was my best friend and that comes from the heart, so the focus should not be so much on the words, if the words are spoken with love and from the heart.

He was right. Who was I to teach my grandfather to be politically correct, while denying somehow the truth of what he was saying. My grandfather was a good man, with a big heart, who would do anything for a friend, anything for a neighbor, including giving that person that last of what he had, even if it meant going without himself.

My grandfather told me about truths, big and small, about how God does not care if you are Democrat or Republican, worker or boss, wealthy or poor, God cares about you being a good person. Acting honest in your business dealings, never cheating anyone, always making sure you are fair, lending a hand, passing a compliment, carrying groceries, loaning without expecting repayment. Giving all that you have, asking for little, paying your bills, carrying no debt.

He said God does not care if you have a lot of things or a big house, or a few things and a small house, as long as you take care of everyone inside and pay all the bills for each. Don't act lofty, because you will always have less than someone. Don't act intimidated, because you will always have more than someone. Don't expect more than whatever God gives you each day. Go out and work hard, do your best, piece it all together and have gratitude for all those blessings- being able to work, having the capacity to accomplish much, showing appreciation that you are managing with God's gifts.

I was in a bike accident and my then nine year old face was a mess, a mass of blood and cuts. Permanent scarring, the doctor gravely stated. She will never be pretty again, my grandfather lamented to my mother, privately, in the living room, intended to be shielded from my ears. But, I heard. And,

I thought to myself, pretty? He thinks I am pretty? I went to the mirror and assessed the damage. My face was now swollen beyond recognition and places on my face were raw, deep to cauliflower tissue.

Each day I smoothed a thin layer of Vaseline over the raw, exposed skin, wiping away dust and dirt from the day prior. Pretty? I did not see it. But, I would not have the designated devastating scars. Some nerve damage, no broken bones, just pale white smooth skin. As long as he thought I was beautiful, or rather pretty, he said. Okay, something to chew on along with his gift of an extra large bag of peanut M&Ms.

There were always stories of his strength and courage, his devotion to family and friends. One story is that he caught the chicken coop, braced his body between it and his little girl, my mother at age three, held up the massive weight until she scurried to safety and others came to help move the coop upright again. That is it around our house, only a few sketchy details. It must have been bad because that is how these things go. If it is bad, there are hushed voices, few facts, jaws snap shut upon questioning, you are better off to silently listen but pretend you are preoccupied in hopes they forget a child is in the room, as they recount the details to a fellow farmer.

My understanding is that when the three young men tried to take his wallet and hence his money, he resisted, no, rather, he fought back. Fought the three men, still lost the money, but held tight to his dignity. An important matter. It scared us deeply. He was brave. And stupid, we told him. We hugged him tight, and worried for his age and how thugs target elderly and other weakened populations, reflected from a distance on whether he looked vulnerable, whether he needed bolstering of some sort. What that would look like, I have no idea.

Pride is what he carried mostly. Integrity in each pocket. A slew of honesty and reliability. He had a bellyful of experience and understanding. A head for kindness and equity. I hear they escaped with his wallet, a bit of pride, of which he has plenty, a large amount of cash, no credit cards, he never believed in credit, and left his ego with a bit of bruising, some physical bruising as well. Not that he would ever complain about that.

Nope, he would not complain about anything, so I never knew him to want or to need. I never knew him to be lacking in anything- from friendship to money to courage.

It is especially difficult then, when a figure of such countenance and strength declines in health, and the inevitable is nearing. For me, denial was the best course of action. Consumed by his personality, will, strength of character, and expecting that to trump all maladies.

Psalm 25:20-21 Guard my life and rescue me; do not let me be put to shame, for I take refuge in you. May integrity and uprightness protect me, because my hope, LORD, is in you.

It was clear that he was very ill, in fact, dying. But, I was a child, his grandchild, and not in any hurry to let him go, at least not in any timely manner. Not knowing what to say, whether to acknowledge what I tried to deny, what I could do to help, whether anything I did or said would make him better or worse, I teetered between the obvious and that tiny speck of hope.

I remember telling him to eat his applesauce as I was leaving his house near the end and feeling incredibly guilty and stupid both for expecting him to be able to eat and for asking him to do so. I could see his struggle and somehow felt that if he ate something it would buy him that much more time-selfishly I clung weakly to that small hope.

At night, I laid in bed and I prayed for his health, for forever, for my own self interest in having, holding, keeping my grandfather. I did not know how to deal with him dying.

And then, I remember, we were driving past wheat fields, an unfamiliar landscape, to a large, white farmhouse, nestled in the landscape. My cousin stood at the doorway with a large bouquet of blood red roses. Boy, aren't those beautiful roses, I remarked as I walked past her and into the house. I woke and looked at my digital clock next to my bed. Three thirty in the morning. What an odd dream, I thought, remembering the vividness of the roses, the starkness of the fields, the familiarity of the farmhouse I did not recognize. I wondered what made me wake up so abruptly from my dream. I went back to sleep and woke to my alarm at six thirty.

Rather than starting my normal Sunday morning routine, showering and dressing for church, I sat on the bed, a bit listless and subdued, thoughtful. After a short period of time, my mom burst into my room, preoccupied and frenzied as she told me not to get ready for church. She stopped abruptly and stared at me, sitting on my bed, still in my pajamas.

Well, don't get ready for church she said again, staring quizzically at me, because I had not even started to get ready.

Your grandfather died, she said. We are driving to Michigan for the funeral. She was gone as swiftly as she entered.

Yes, I know, I thought.

Did I know? How did I know?

We drove from our home in Ohio to his home in Michigan, hear where I had grown up, attended the funeral, the ceremony at the gravesite, and anguished in the unfamiliar pain of loss juxtaposed against the distinctive, recognizable scent of the dark red roses covering my grandfather's casket, his and my grandmother's favorite.

Then, we drove through unfamiliar landscape, past wheat fields, to a large, white farmhouse, nestled in the landscape. My cousin stood at the doorway with a large bouquet of blood red roses. Boy, aren't those beautiful roses, I remarked, as I walked past her and into the house. I stopped abruptly remembering my dream of just a few days prior.

My grandfather died at three thirty that Sunday morning of my dream. My great uncle, Richard, his brother, woke at three thirty and saw my grandfather standing at the end of his bed. He ran through his house, the white farmhouse, waking everyone and telling them of his vision. Everyone told him to calm down and go back to sleep, that it was just a dream. My grandmother, asleep at her own house, also woke at three thirty and saw her husband, my grandfather, standing at the end of her bed. I had been dreaming the events after the funeral and woke at the time of his death.

It scared me, knowing ahead of time, but not realizing the significance of my dream, yet feeling it was significant, and not putting it together until that déjà vu moment after the funeral. Why a special message for me ahead of the others or did everyone get the same advanced warning and elect not to share or brush it off as insignificant or simply not remember?

I think God wanted to let me know ahead of time, a pleasant dream to carry me through, to help me understand and appreciate the physical but not spiritual loss. And, my grandfather dared not leave without checking on his brother and wife first. That is who he was. I could see him headed off to heaven but straining just a bit to wave goodbye first. They would be upset they couldn't be there in those final moments, to see him off, make sure he did not suffer, reassure themselves he was okay at the end. He would tell them all of that was okay as he was leaving. A considered attempt to alleviate some of their worry.

He died owing nothing, no regrets, nothing left unsaid, because he said it, demonstrated it, and lived it, each and every day.

My grandfather, my hero- who taught me that pretty means special and valued, special means important and of consequence, important mandates responsibility, and responsibility means integrity in all matters of conduct. Thirty plus years ago, my grandfather died. And, even today, I would say he is/was one of the most influential people in my life. He took care of others with candor and deliberateness, gratitude, thoughtfulness. He was principled. He taught me integrity, in life and in death. And because he stopped by to show me his ticket to heaven.

Integrity,
a pure and honest heart,
lasts beyond death.

God is with us; God is the constant, in life and in death.

We can selfishly pray to delay death, but death itself does not bring closure; who we are in life carries us through death, on our journey to heaven.

Luke 8:4-15 While a large crowd was gathering and people were coming to Jesus from town after town, he told this parable: "A farmer went out to sow his seed. As he was scattering the seed, some fell along the path; it was trampled on, and the birds ate it up. Some fell on the rocky ground, and when it came up, the plants were withered because they had no moisture. Other seed fell among thorns, which grew up with it and choked the plants. Still other seed fell on good soil. It came up and yielded a crop, a hundred times more than was sown." When he said this, he called out, "Whoever has ears to hear, let them hear." His disciples asked him what this parable meant. He said, "The knowledge of the secrets of the kingdom of God has been given to you, but to others I speak in parables, so that, though seeing, they may not see; though hearing, they may not understand."

"This is the meaning of the parable: The seed is the word of God. Those along the path are the ones who hear, and then the devil comes and takes away the word from their hearts, so that they may not believe and be saved. Those on the rocky ground are the ones who receive the word with joy when they hear it, but they have no root. They believe for a while, but in the time of testing they fall away. The seed that fell among thorns stands for those who hear, but as they go on their way they are choked by life's worries, riches and pleasures, and they do not mature. But the seed on good soil stands for those with a noble and good heart, who hear the word, retain it, and by persevering produce a crop."

THEN, HOPE

SPIRITUAL GUIDES, ANGELS, MENTORS, AND FRIENDS

THERE ARE PEOPLE THAT YOU meet, or that simply cross your path briefly, that touch you in a way that is profound and lasting, whether they knew or intended it or not. Perhaps it is intentional, guides sent with messages, angels coaxing a new direction, preparation for a future day or that day, that moment, that split second in time.

You feel it, you know it, even if you are not quite sure exactly what it is. But, as it warms you and carries you and comforts you and in that blanket and cloak of protection, you no longer need an explanation.

And, you know, clearly, without rationale, that there is more at work than just the moment, the words, the accidental or purposeful meeting. God is present, palpable.

A lesson, a sign, a gift, warning, encouragement, prospective, perspective, light.

And, sometimes the message is not flattering, not all warm and fuzzy, but relevant, stinging, poignant, accurate, needed, and in our recognition, welcomed.

For example, Lisa.

As an undergraduate at Bowling Green State University, I was always running late to my early morning Psychology class. And, Lisa was so sweet to always save me a seat near the front of the lecture hall. Breathless, I would drop down into the seat next to hers, having ran all the way across campus, dressed quickly in sweatshirt and jeans, hair thrown in a sloppy ponytail. She was always nicely dressed, everything matching, something crisp about her look, as if all of her clothes were brand new.

One day, as I slid into my seat at the last minute, tired, grouchy, and a bit irritated by my sloppy appearance next to hers, I said a bit sharply, you always look nice, and I don't.

She was startled and her face clouded a bit. All of my clothes are new, she stammered, a fire in the apartment next to mine, all of my belongings were smoke damaged. Her voice trailed off. The Psychology lecture began. I slid further down in my seat. How rude was I? Envy, jealously? Of someone who lost everything in a fire?

I never saw her again. Never. She was absent from class after that. Dropped out? A figment of my imagination? Had she been there? Lesson learned. The mentor has moved on. Sometimes the gift, the sign, is a kick in the behind. And needed.

Painful lessons. Sometimes the best gifts are nestled in the most difficult, awkward, unlikely, unsuspecting situations. The constant is always humility, presence, and a good dose of hope. After all, it is the recognition that we just had a glimpse, a peek at God's presence, that propels us forward to carry on, to acknowledge that at least we are considered worthy of the lesson, no matter how elementary.

God is present, always, and that presence palpable much of the time. Sometimes, when we least expect it. And, oh so clearly demonstrated in the goodness of angels.

Faith, now hope.

Lessons of hope in spiritual guides, angels, mentors, and friends.

Psalm 33:22 May your unfailing love be with us, LORD, even as we put our hope in you.

Hope Soup

Luke 21:1-4 As Jesus looked up, he saw the rich putting their gifts into the temple treasury. He also saw a poor widow put in two very small copper coins. "Truly I tell you," he said, "this poor widow has put in more than all the others. All these people gave their gifts out of their wealth; but she out of her poverty put in all she had to live on."

WE LIVED IN A HOTEL for six weeks after our house burned down in the wildfires. Then, one year in a rental after that. Our friends moved out of their home and into an investment property they had purchased, to allow us to rent their home and, thereby, be close to our children's elementary school. We embarked on the process of rebuilding right away, making and submitting plans to our homeowners association, submitting claims to our insurance company, then decided we were better off to purchase an extensively fire damaged house in our same neighborhood to have stability and permanence more quickly for our children.

During those six weeks in the hotel, we ate a lot of fast food, helped the children with homework at a very small table, our college son slept on the floor when he visited, we made personal property lists for our insurance company, and struggled to keep our pets, cat and rat, separated.

Every little thing seemed like such a struggle- a child asking for a ruler, stapler, scotch tape, pen/pencil, colored pencil, colored paper just to complete one homework assignment (and we have four kids!), getting the mail, traversing the complex insurance claim morass, dealing with mortgage company inquiries, getting refills on prescriptions that burnt up, lacking the luxury of shopping clearance and sales because needs of clothing and office were immediate, new checks, duplicate bills, transferring our phone number, cancelling cable and sewer. And, sometimes the people involved were as challenging as the problem- pharmacies did not want to refill prescriptions, the mortgage company thought the mortgage should simply be paid in full, immediately. And, emails never received obviously went unanswered, each creating a mini-drama.

Succulent plants that survived the fire were dug up and stolen off our burned up lot. River rock taken too. And rakes, shovels, garden hoses purchased to hose off blackened trees and driveway. Anything we purchased to restore some order to our lot was taken, replaced, and taken again.

At the same time, people stepped up in remarkable ways to assist us. They simply showed up unannounced. Helpful. Caring. Sincere. Wanting to know how to help. Offering free labor to sift through the rubble, donating clothing and household goods. Sometimes well-intended people donated things like bookcases, for books we no longer had, to house in a hotel room along with children, a cat, and a pet rat? It was clearly difficult for people to grasp an absence of all things, such that storage is really not an issue at this point. We would chuckle, speaking of our now very open floor plan and neighboring fire families put up amusing signs giving thanks for "No more termites!"

The mother of our son's friend, someone I had never met, called me one day. She introduced herself and asked if we would like some homemade soup to enjoy at our hotel. Homemade chicken noodle soup.

The hotel suite had a small refrigerator, microwave, and even a very small stove. But, with four kids and the burners so close to the refrigerator and one child autistic, cooking was not a safe option. Eating unprocessed food was so important to his diet, a luxury abandoned when we fled the fire to the safety of a hotel. Yes, yes, I answered, and explained to her how valuable a contribution to his wellbeing she would be making and plus how appreciative all of us would be to eat something homemade. Even the kids had grown tired of McDonald's and pizza.

Michelle brought us a large container of homemade chicken noodle soup, big noodles, chunks of carrot and chicken, celery, just the right seasoning. Not that we would have been picky. At all. But, that said, this was some good soup. Medicinal, full of love, caring. We felt it. We ate it. We truly appreciated the soup and her and her sacrifice in making us a home cooked meal.

A few days later, she called to check in and see if we enjoyed the soup. Yes, yes, I answered. Thank you, thank you oh so much.

Would you like more, she asked.

Yes, yes. But, only if it is not too much trouble. I hesitated. We really would appreciate more, but only if it is not too much trouble.

Of course not. I would love to, she answered. This Thursday. I will stop by with more soup on Thursday.

Thursday came and went and with trying to gain some semblance of normalcy living in a hotel room, we did not completely notice though in the back of my mind I thought of her and her generosity. Friday, no soup. That is okay, I thought to myself. How generous she has been already. I will put it out of my mind.

Saturday morning, a knock on the door and a frenzied, friendly, Michelle popped in with an even bigger container of homemade soup. I am so sorry, she explained. I should not have told you I would return on Thursday. I had to wait until I got paid on Friday in order to have the money to purchase the ingredients for the soup.

I will never forget that moment. The realization that someone you barely know is giving you all the extra they have, and probably quite a bit more. Dipping into their resources, living check to check, modest means, employed but just scraping by, like so many people, each and every day. She gave us everything and then spent her time cooking, wrapping it with a bow, sealing it with love, sending it off to us, the family of a friend of her young son.

And it carried us and nourished us and lifted our spirits. The gift great, the care profound.

We met people like that all throughout our recovery. People that would give you all that they had, and more if you let them. Angels, guides, mentors, friends, God's gift, each day, each hour, availing, arms stretched out, beckoning. Hope. In a container of soup. Warmed. Homemade hope.

You feel it, you know it, even if you are not quite sure exactly what it is. But, as it warms you and carries you and comforts you and in that blanket and cloak of protection, you no longer need an explanation.

And, you know, clearly, without rationale, that there is more at work than just the moment, the words, the accidental or purposeful meeting. God is present, palpable.

Encouragement, light. Hope, in soup.

The purest dose of hope is granted when someone gives you all that they have to give.

We can serve and be served. Witness and bear witness. Any time. Any place. Using the tools of desire and heart.

Acts 20:35 "In everything I did, I showed you that by this kind of hard work we must help the weak, remembering the words the Lord Jesus himself said: 'It is more blessed to give than to receive.'"

CRIPPLED?

*Hebrews 12:1-3 Therefore, since we are surrounded by such a great cloud
of witnesses, let us throw off everything that hinders and the sin that so
easily entangles. And let us run with perseverance the race marked out
for us, fixing our eyes on Jesus, the pioneer and perfecter of faith. For the
joy set before him he endured the cross, scorning its shame, and sat down
at the right hand of the throne of God. Consider him who endured such
opposition from sinners, so that you will not grow weary and lose heart.*

M Y VERY FIRST FRIEND, ROSIE, was seriously crippled with a rare
incurable degenerative disease. Our friendship, unmarred by her
physical limitations, lasted just a few fleeting years until she deteriorated
unto death. She made a lasting impression on me because we shared so
much with each other during that time, intellectually and emotionally,
our exchanges never reduced to a discussion of her numerous doctor
appointments and increasing physical limitations.

I have always been comfortable around populations of mentally
challenged, physically challenged, and ill individuals, having volunteered
at nursing homes, hospitals, group homes, and at unique facilities providing
services to men and women, young and old, joined together by common need
or purpose. I read to a blind professor, taught adults with cerebral palsy to
ride horses, swimming lessons to elderly, coordinated activities for mentally

challenged children. One summer I worked at a camp for abused children, building a shed, pouring a concrete patio, repairing a fence. I connected with special needs children using puppets, theatre, singing, poetry, stories, and one-on-one individual exchanges.

When I first began volunteering, the correct terminology was handicapped persons but now acknowledge challenged as a more politically correct designation. Irrespective, inside the shell housing each person is someone good, interesting, intelligent, wanting, longing, yearning for acceptance, relationship, touch, hug, a shared laugh, a genuine connection.

Every volunteer opportunity I have had has taught me more and given more to me than I have offered. I am blessed for every one of those experiences.

Or, perhaps I thought I was comfortable, until he approached me. His arms were bolstered by intricate crutches, his lifeless legs dead weight behind him. He moved one arm toward me, then another, then dragged his legs underneath him to move slowly forward. His face revealed considerable strain with each awkward, jerky movement.

It was Valentine's Day. I was sitting by myself in the cafeteria adjoining my college dorm. I had just broken up with my boyfriend, or rather, he with me. So predictable. We had a volatile, unhealthy, toxic, back and forth, immature relationship peppered with moments of connection, introspection and intimacy. When we would start to get close, he pushed me away, not desiring a commitment, not wanting to validate the relationship.

I was trapped, locked in a war of mind versus emotion, common sense versus wistful fiction, a fly tapping incessantly at self imposed glass, the door open just feet away. And, so I engaged in the dance, of theatre and poetry, more tragedy than drama, more Shakespeare and Legend than Homer. Thus, I sat, alone, in the cafeteria bustling with life, feeling dramatically sorry for myself.

Matthew 23:12 For those who exalt themselves will be humbled, and those who humble themselves will be exalted.

The man approached me, having traversed the entire length of the room to speak directly to me, beads of sweat on his forehead from the exertion of his efforts. He leaned toward me, balanced precariously on his crutches, and spoke softly, the words punctuated with clarity and kindness, "A girl as pretty as you, should not be sitting alone on Valentine's Day." With that, he smiled and turned, and began the long trek back to his seat.

I sat there stunned. And embarrassed. Was my sadness that apparent, the recent dramatic exchange with my boyfriend so visible? How does one wear self-pity? How pathetic was I to the world around me? How many times had I asked God about this relationship, asked for help or guidance, knowing the answer but not wanting to hear?

The exchange was brief, so long ago, a blip on the screen, but so meaningful to me, even still today. A very sweetly delivered swift kick in the behind.

As between us, surely, as I sat there, I was the only one crippled.

There are signs all around us, pointing us in the right direction, saving us from ourselves, reminding us of what we acknowledge we should already know.

We are crippled without humility.

Sometimes the best gifts are nestled in the most difficult, awkward, unlikely, unsuspecting situations. The constant is always humility, presence, and a good dose of hope. Again, it is the recognition that we just had a glimpse, a peek at God's presence, that propels us forward to carry on, to acknowledge that at least, swimming in humility, we are considered worthy of the lesson, no matter how elementary. And, no matter how many lessons we need.

People enter our lives and bring us messages, lessons, connection, love. And, sometimes the message, deserved and appropriate, is simply a bath in humility.

Philippians 2:3-4 Do nothing out of selfish ambition or vain conceit. Rather, in humility value others above yourselves, not looking to your own interests but each of you to the interests of the others.

Roadblock

I Thessalonians 5:12-18 Now we ask you, brothers and sisters to acknowledge those who work hard among you, who care for you in the Lord and who admonish you. Hold them in the highest regard in love because of their work. Live in peace with each other. And we urge you, brothers and sisters, warn those who are idle and disruptive, encourage the disheartened, help the weak, be patient with everyone. Make sure that nobody pays back wrong for wrong, but always strive to do what is good for each other and for everyone else.

Rejoice always, pray continually, give thanks in all circumstances; for this is God's will for you in Christ Jesus.

People cloud our day, all the spots are taken in the parking lot and we drive around and around looking for an available spot, the clerk is not available when you have a question, the phone rings as you rush out the door, an accident has traffic backed up for miles, the delivery is late, the waitress is cool, the soup is cold, someone is talking way too loudly on a cell phone, the neighboring table is harboring a complicated argument that wafts over to you like cigarette smoke.

There are a lot of people prospectively in our way. Or not. Moving through challenges, maybe trying to overcome, maybe stuck, but not our struggle to bear.

Do we own our interdependence, that they are part of our equation, at least for that day? Do we value the interaction, seek the connection, look for the meaning, acknowledge the contribution, note the role we play for each other, the potential we bring to each other's lives?

I was driving, the thousandth time down the same stretch of road, rushing, always, because I have so many obligations, kids, objectives, so few hours to squeeze it all in. Always someone slow, blocking my way, slowing to turn but not quite sure where they want to turn, driving in the fast lane on the highway but going far below the speed limit, or talking or texting, weaving, making me fearful to pass.

She had to have been at least eighty, her eyes barely cleared the steering wheel, hunched over, peering into the street ahead. I could tell all of this from behind her because I was driving as near to her as one could manage without placing her within my car itself. I don't normally follow that closely but she was really starting to exasperate me. She approached the intersection, green light, hesitation, now yellow, she stopped. I stopped behind her, close at hand. Irritated. The light changed to red. A long red. Finally, the light changed back to green but she did not move. She looked long and hard to the right and left, left and right, but did not go.

I waited. She waited. I waited some more.

Suddenly, a semi, driving at top speed down the street we were poised to turn onto to, ran his red light and rumbled loudly past the two of us, us stopped with a green light in our direction. I blinked. The roar of the engine still audible in the distance. Now, she slowly and deliberately pulled into the intersection. I did as well- after many long looks right then left, left then right.

Then, I said thank you. To her and to God.

Was she there, in that moment, in that second, for a purpose? Luck? Coincidence? Intentional?

Patience. Breathe. A moment could change everything and every moment is a new opportunity.

If we pray, we pray that God remove the roadblock and let us go on our way. Do we pray our thanks, our gratitude; do we see the protection, help, the blessing? How many people enter our lives daily and provide protection, shield, just slow us down. And, do we actually see them or just judge them as a roadblock to our day.

What if I stopped for a moment to consider the relationship between me and them? Our interdependence. Our relationship together in this space and time. Consider for a moment that they are in front of me for a purpose, the purpose of slowing me down. Preventing me from racing so fast that when the truck a half mile ahead drops a ladder in the road, I am not the recipient. Slowing me down such that when that car merges into my lane with no care for my position, I am able to slam on my brakes with sufficient time. What if it is purposeful, that person being there at that exact moment in time?

Luke 6:37-28 *"Do not judge, and you will not be judged. Do not condemn, and you will not be condemned. Forgive, and you will be forgiven. Give, and it will be given to you. A good measure, pressed down, shaken together and running over, will be poured into your lap. For with the measure you use, it will be measured to you."*

How would my feelings toward a young mother blocking the grocery aisle, harshly scolding her five year old, change if I knew that, just days before, her husband learned his overseas military assignment was extended by another six months? Would I stop and tell her that I have had hard days too and reach out to her as a mom and neighbor?

Would I patiently wait my turn or grant a nod of approval to that very large, multi-hundreds of pounds couple, dominating the salad bar buffet, if I knew they just lost nearly one hundred pounds each and are continuing to strictly adhere to their diets by eating large amounts of salad? Would I offer my heartfelt congratulations or measure them by their place in the struggle?

If I knew that the neighbor who scowls at my children when they run into his yard to retrieve a stray ball tragically lost his children years before make me look at him differently?

When do we stop seeing others as obstacles- to our speed, our goals, our plan, our needs, our self interest and recognize them as partners in synchronized life dance as predictable and constant as the tide reaching, lapping at the shore? At what point do we recognize that we are all in the same boat, rowing, whether together, in sync, orchestrated or not.

When my husband, Mike, was in college, he scheduled an end of the year mountain climbing trip to climb Mount Rainier. The travel agent mistakenly scheduled his flight for a day earlier than planned. Mike had a final exam scheduled that day, but the flight was non-refundable and could not be changed to another date. He had been training and planning for his mountain climbing trip for months. So, Mike missed his final exam, took an incomplete in the class, and made up the exam at a later date. The flight from Chicago to Seattle was uneventful and he enjoyed a memorable mountain climbing experience.

However, the flight Mike wanted to take, the one scheduled one day later that would have allowed him to fit into his schedule the final exam and the mountain climbing trip, was not uneventful. Shortly after takeoff, an engine fell off the plane, the plane crashed and everyone on board the plane died on impact.

We never know what the entire puzzle looks like, even if we think we know what our individual pieces represent. How everything fits together may take a lifetime to comprehend. But, for all our planning and schedules, priorities and deadlines, it is the nothingness of any given day, the ordinary, regular, uneventful day that we discard and take for granted. And, we take for granted that all went well because we cannot see that cautious driver, the mistake by the travel agent, may be the greatest gift of all. That may be the very day, hour, moment to give the greatest thanks. Because nothing happened.

Rather than being frustrated at not getting everything done, rushing through every day, planning and scheduling, trying to fit it all, contemplate those roadblocks and say thanks. Those mentors, angels, and guides may be working hard to protect us from worse, keep us on the right path, push us down another road, correct our wayward wandering, and recenter us to move forward in due time. God's presence, a step removed, through spiritual messengers, allowing us to be absent much of the time, when our presence might serve to steer us toward gratitude.

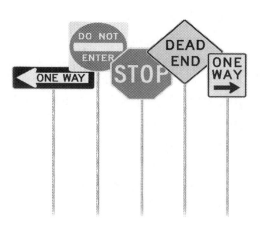

Roadblocks are placed before us as opportunities to stay safe, to reflect, to pause, to contemplate, before we make our next move.

Everyone is part of our equation, we are interdependent.

Colossians 1:9-14 For this reason, since the day we heard about you, we have not stopped praying for you. We continually ask God to fill you with the knowledge of his will through all the wisdom and understanding that the Spirit gives, so that you may live a life worthy of the Lord and please him in every way: bearing fruit in every good work, growing in the knowledge of God, being strengthened with all power according to his glorious might so that you may have great endurance and patience, and giving joyful thanks to the Father, who has qualified you to share in the inheritance of his holy people in the kingdom of light. For he has rescued us from the dominion of darkness and brought us into the kingdom of the Son he loves, in whom we have redemption, the forgiveness of sins.

LETTER TO THE WOMEN OF CIRCLE 6

Isaiah 43:18-19 "Forget the former things; do not dwell on the past. See, I am doing a new thing! Now it springs up; do you not perceive it? I am making a way in the wilderness and streams in the wasteland."

MY SISTER, PAM, TOLD THE women's group at her church in Ohio about the loss of our home in the San Diego wildfires. The women decided to make and personalize Christmas ornaments as a gift to our family at the holidays.

These women gave me a gift I could have never anticipated and did not realize even as it was first offered. It touched me deeply to experience their thoughtfulness and attention to the details of my family as captured in little, brightly painted ornaments.

The following is my letter of thanks to this group of women I have never met.

> Dear Circle 6/Women of Fairmont Church:
>
> I just wanted to write to say thank you. You don't know me and I don't know any of you. After I lost my home in the San Diego wildfires in October 2007, all of you chipped in to make or buy Christmas ornaments for our family. And,

to be honest, I cannot even remember if I said thank you at that time. You see, Christmas in December 2007 was just a blur. I remember putting up a tree just a day or two before Christmas and taking it down soon after. I just wanted to get through the holidays, and if I didn't have children, I would have probably skipped those rituals all together.

There are things that I miss from our house burning down. I miss the baby books, mostly because I am so bad at remembering who weighed what and the first word each one said. Not because I don't care or cannot remember them as babies, but rather because those aren't the kinds of things I noticed or cared about at the time, but maybe down the road they will want to know. I never counted fingers and toes in the moments after they were born; I just looked each one in the eyes and marveled that they had made the journey safely from God to me.

I miss the Barbie doll clothes that my Grandmother hand-made for me. My Grandmother is still around and doing quite well for her age, but I recognize the amount of work each piece must have took, and with her rheumatoid arthritis, there is no way she could ever replicate them again. And, the clothes were so incredible. My Grandmother, who grew up in rural Illinois, one of seven children, with little but the dirt on their plot of land, had an indescribable eye for fashion. She handmade a wedding dress and veil, gowns with tiny beads, matching purses and shoes, lace underneath, layers, taffeta and velvets.

I miss my honeymoon pictures and the photo albums from when Mike and I first met because I want to have something to remind me of camping and hiking and all the silly things we did twenty-some years ago. I miss the handmade Mother's Day cards from my four boys, all tied with a satin ribbon in the top right-hand drawer of my dresser. I am anxious without the records I meticulously kept documenting my son's medical care for his four brain surgeries, treatment by three different surgeons, fifteen doctors, school records and medication records, notes regarding his progress, insurance papers. I miss the piano music I composed while in college and my poems from second grade on. I miss Karrson's drawings, especially the one he colored in crayon entitled "Birth" that I had framed and hanging in my living room.

And, I miss my Christmas ornaments. Yes, Christmas ornaments. That's what brings me to you.

You see, I always decorated the Christmas tree, always, whether anyone else joined me or not, as a child and as an adult. I had Norman Rockwell ornaments that I was collecting, each one a miniature masterpiece. I had the little mouse peaking out of a red stocking that my friend gave to me when we were in fifth grade. There were ornaments made by each of the kids when they were in preschool and the ornaments signifying Baby's first Christmas and other special occasions. There were wooden handmade ornaments from Mike's mother for each of us to represent something we were interested in that year, a sport, musical instrument, or hobby. There were shiny ball ornaments that we had forever, not that attractive, and we would usually break one or two each year, but we packed them up after each Christmas along with all the other precious ornaments, and tacky as they were, we liked them. There was a star for the top of the tree that would blink. And, a bear in an igloo that lit up, strings of lights, icicles, a sled, a gold angel, crystal heart and bell, and a silly pickle.

I miss the handmade ornaments from my mother. Mom made little cloth animal ornaments. The spots on the giraffe would sometimes be heart-shaped, or the eyes of the elephant would have eyelashes. She sewed our name on the ornament itself, and we always had to hang our own ornaments on the tree each year. Mom and I were never close, except when it came to the Christmas ornaments. Even when I was small, I could pull out an ornament and say to her, "This one is really good, Mom" and show her something she had made and she would remember it and talk about why she made that particular one that way or why a certain person received that one. I loved those ornaments and through each one, through the recognition of the time and care and thoughtfulness it took to make each one, I could love her too.

And, so, Christmas is hard, because of the ornaments. I don't want to open those boxes of carefully wrapped ornaments and not see the ones that she made for me. And, so, this year I was dreading it, dreading decorating the Christmas tree, something I always did and always wanted to do. I stuck the tree in a room far away and I waited a long time to decorate it.

Just days before Christmas I opened the ornament box and found so many tiny and magical ornaments looking back at me; ornaments from all of you to us, one with my son's preschool picture, several with our names, little snowmen, families, all smiling, sparkly and special. I started to hang them up quickly, but then I couldn't help but notice all the little details on each one and I couldn't help but recognize the time and care and thoughtfulness it took to make or pick out each one.

It is not ever about the things, is it? Rather, it is about the ability of the things to bring us together. That is what I miss and that is what makes it better. And, so, I just wanted to write to say thank you.

Much love,

Karen

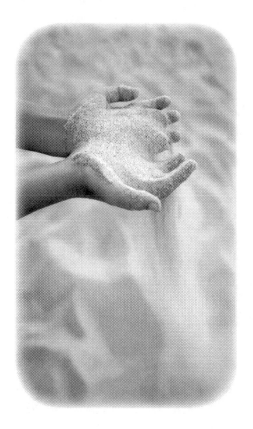

Letting go of things from the past
creates space for new connections, people, memories,
reflecting new and expanded relationships.

We can choose to surround ourselves with objects that exemplify expressions of love and hope. Recognize the expressions of love and hope in the objects we are granted.

Job 11:13-18 Yet if you devote your heart to him and stretch out your hands to him, If you put away the sin that is in your land and allow no evil to dwell in your tent Then, free of fault, you will lift up your face; you will stand firm and without fear. You will surely forget your trouble, recalling it only as waters gone by. Life will be brighter than noonday, and darkness will become like morning. You will be secure, because there is hope; you will look about you and take your rest in safety.

3RD AND ASH

Romans 5:1-5 Therefore, since we have been justified through faith, we have peace with God through our Lord Jesus Christ, through whom we have gained access by faith into this grace in which we now stand. And we boast in the hope of the glory of God. Not only so, but we also glory in our sufferings, because we know that suffering produces perseverance; perseverance, character; and character, hope. And hope does not put us to shame, because God's love has been poured out into our hearts through the Holy Spirit, who has been given to us.

THERE ARE PEOPLE THAT YOU meet, or that simply cross your path briefly, that touch you in a way that is profound and lasting, whether they knew and intended it or not. Perhaps it is intentional, guides sent with messages, angels coaxing a new direction, or preparation for a future day. A lesson, sign, a gift, warning, encouragement, prospective, perspective, light. And, sometimes the message is not flattering, not all warm and fuzzy, but relevant, stinging, poignant, accurate, needed, and in our recognition, welcomed.

God's presence is evidenced in charity, compassion, understanding, and in our collective humanity. Our ability to come together to see ourselves and others at the core of our being as the same. And, sometimes that recognition is only realized by our own or our witness to other's suffering, loss, oppression, grief. In that recognition, there is a collective consciousness of need and compassion. From that collective consciousness, hope is exemplified.

Even our collective frustration, our anger, serves to propel us to disengage and meet immediate needs or to engage and seek better, all a culmination of our undying, inexhaustible hope. Continuous political wrangling, no matter your side of the aisle, drains and depletes our national psyche, resulting in a protective dissociation, though we are invested, wholly, in every issue of the day. We live those bantered and battered statistics of economic instability and market volatility reduced to sound bites to produce thirty second commercials.

Properties, hastily vacated, bear witness of children, scraps of abandoned toys, school supplies spilled onto neglected carpet squares, displays scars of care and anger, thoughtfully stenciled pink unicorns and upgraded kitchen hardware amidst holes punched deliberately into drywall, expletive woven graffiti messages punctuate the living room, cheap layer of primer no match for blackened cast of frustration. Bank owned, the real estate listing announces ominously. Contingent on bank approval another announces feeble, crippled attempt at short sale, the relative from across the tracts, though both would argue the other on the wrong side of the map. Furniture marred by a hasty exit pale next to scars of former students all-in on this round of the housing poker roulette game.

Sitting in chairs at 3rd and Ash in downtown San Diego, a couple, man and woman, stake a spot on the cement, next to the pay by the hour parking lot. A tarp next to them covers a pile of belongings. They huddle in the early morning chill and chatter back and forth about politics and people as the downtown crowd bustles by just a few feet away. Smiling at each other warmly, they play a competitive card game, slapping a thigh and laughing loudly as they trump the other. Nightly, they slink beneath the tarp, nestled on top of the chairs and scraps, drawing heat from the strength of their relationship.

In San Diego County, over two thousand homeless children slip between foster homes or adorn the streets, invisible, painted with acid rain, clothed in remnant scraps of vintage resale clothing, two sizes too something, off kilter, thin, waif-like, modelesque. Strategically indifferent, they exist throughout the day, and consider it an accomplishment to be ignored.

The stress of the compacted strain of banned plastic grocery bags, wholly inadequate for quelling the face of America's disposal. The beach is closed again because much needed rain washes over the arid land and runs off flooding storm drains flushing waste to the ocean, defecating on our food supply, tourists dissuaded by caution signs from entering frothy waters dancing against pale blue pristine skies.

A short distance away the Occupy San Diego movement moves, ebbing and flowing across public space of concourse and civic center, government offices flanking the strategy sessions, or general meetings. They camp and disperse, arrested and questioned, released, challenged, regroup, stand lest they appear to be camping, and camp once more. They wane and thicken, draw together, steadfastly assert they are individuals, the difficulty of communication with authority punctuated by lack of appointed leadership, or ownership of all. They want relief, respite, equity. To know the rules.

Deuteronomy 26:7 "Then we cried out to the Lord, the God of our ancestors, and the Lord heard our voice and saw our misery, toil and oppression."

And, John Steinbeck's *Grapes of Wrath*, warns in prophetic prose:

And the great owners, who must lose their land in an upheaval, the great owners with access to history, with eyes to read history and to know the great fact: when property accumulates in too few hands it is taken away. And that companion fact: when a majority of the people are hungry and cold they will take by force what they need. And the little screaming fact that sounds through all history: repression works only to strengthen and knit the repressed. The great owners ignored the three cries of history. The land fell into fewer hands, the number of dispossessed increased, and every effort of the great owners was directed at repression.

I install an owl box in hopes of exterminating brazen gophers content to flip me off before meandering back to cavernous networks beneath every rose bush, vegetable garden, succulent, and ground cover. Anything healthy is stripped bare or weakened to an unrecognizable state, as the fattened gophers move across the landscape like a plow. The owl finds a mate and soon is raising squawking politician babies that learn to fly far from the roost to hunt in the valley. I am kept awake late into the night by the ruckus and learn that, while implementing such rodent squelching measures is optional, removal of active, sitting senatorial owl boxes is prohibited.

I wonder who, me or neighbor, will be the first to break that law, as sleep deprivation colors obligation. But, soon the brood matures and moves on, leaving the much quieter empty nester parents to carry on. Still, like corporate bankers, the gophers find fertile ground and persevere, buoyed by my efforts to replant, fertilize and repopulate, relying on my replenishing prior to hillside collapse.

Job 35:9 "People cry out under a load of oppression; they plead for relief from the arm of the powerful."

I drive children to and from school, nearly four hours each day. The efforts of those around me in sync or opposed, and I can feel frustration, necessity, urgency, and wonder that they do not sense others around them. Or perhaps civility is not relevant on multilane monstrosities of gray managed traffic lanes. A man on a bridge, contemplating jumping, shuts down rush hour traffic filled with on the edge, just getting by, doing all they can do, heads of household and second job, second income drivers in all directions for nearly nine hours. A truck hauls a Blackhawk helicopter, a dramatic display.

Everything is witnessed through the thick windshield glass, the radio warns of traffic delays, political missteps, posturing and wrangling. I pass it all, nearly a major accident each and every day, corner auctioneers peddling a pose of disparity and need, cardboard sign in hand, backpack, a car nestled a safe distance away, they posture for our attention and we feed the drama, the best actors taking the largest prize. Homeless veterans look at the feet of passerby's and ask for nothing, pride burning their vocal cords silent. In neighboring cars, passengers and drivers text and talk, on cell phones and at each other, arguing, laughing, lecturing, scolding, adult to child, a tween, look of exasperation directed skyward.

Proverbs 22:22-23 Do not exploit the poor because they are poor and do not crush the needy in court, for the LORD WILL TAKE UP THEIR CASE AND WILL EXACT LIFE FOR LIFE.

My golden retriever clamors for my last bite of toast, a habit I should break, but not today. I toss her the small bite and she eagerly snaps it up, salivating over the small bit of toast and peanut butter, a display of the same vigor demonstrated by Mercedes driving Carmel Mountain Costco shoppers vying for tiny samples of canned chicken chili as if she is never fed, oblivious to her widening gait. Her view of the world is narrow as ours expands capturing the fragility of distant country economies, worldwide protests, exposes on the recovery of nations post natural disaster. I cringe and cannot deny my witness to need, entitlement, want, need, greed, selfishness, poverty, despair, and have to own some accountability for engaging or electing to disengage.

I watch as Senator Bernie Sanders argues for the middle class to deafening silence on the chamber floors, a miniscule reaction of a few supportive colleagues in attendance while the twitter world tweets madly for the nine hours he speaks. I am awed as his unflappability and perturbed by the lack of reaction from other elected officials, absence of thoughtful dialogue. Exhausted by the collective extrication of humanity, civility, and absence of any semblance of dignity. Angered by both major parties, disturbed by bickering, intentional desire to obstruct and frustrate any collective movement in any direction, the goal to expand conflict.

Psalm 72:14 *"He will rescue them from oppression and violence, for precious is their blood in his sight."*

Meanwhile, police stoically hose down the faces of kneeling UC students with pepper spray, coloring all breathable air with burning, manufactured, poison. I watch, appalled, yet my phone rings incessantly with ominous robocalls request confirmation of the desire of the public for continued conflict and cheerful manned calls requesting campaign contributions casting a strange hue of disconnect between those that have, are, could be, and would not want to even if they could. While Penn State trustees investigate Penn State trustees, oversight by a former FBI head, to assess allegations of sexual abuse against children, while panicked alumni and students blinded by idol worship text a vote for the favorite crooner and pad the campaigns of programs purporting to assist low income disadvantaged youth.

Romans 8:24-25 *For in this hope we were saved. But hope that is seen is no hope at all. Who hopes for what they already have? But if we hope for what we do not yet have, we wait for it patiently.*

And, I am proud to live in America, despite it all. Where the cloak of the mighty, loftily, clad hero worship is still penetrable, homeless teens are not all trafficked as prostitutes but still have a chance of becoming pop star icon or everyday consumer, pepper sprayed students are hailed as victims and police are put on administrative leave, the 99% consciously switch from BOA to credit unions and force the banks to withdraw plans of new fees, where people can say enough and camp on the steps of government and while pundits allege no impact, no feeling, no change, no effect, all of America watches if both through wide open eye gawking and clenched teeth, asking- is this me? A dialogue demanded, perpetuated, no longer stifled. And, homeless couples stake a place in the center of downtown and are not harassed to move along, nothing to see here folks, look the other way.

When I take a sweater to her, they barely break stride in their impassioned discussion but turn to say a quick and gracious, thank you, God bless you, as I, in turn, take my place back in metal encasement to resume my calculated, hostage to the clock, lengthy drive. Deliberately and consciously, they occupy San Diego. I have but a shred of hope remaining, but it is in them that I am hopeful. And, I smile.

My wish for me and for you is to ameliorate frustration with courage. For, to have courage, you have to have hope. And to have hope, you have to believe. You have to believe there is something more, some humanity that ties us all together and keeps us whole.

God's presence is evidenced in our humanity, our ability to see ourselves and each other as one.

When we see each other through pain, loss and suffering, frustration and anger, there is a collective consciousness of compassion.

From that collective consciousness, there is hope.

Romans 15:13 May the God of hope fill you with all joy and peace as you trust in him, so that you may overflow with hope by the power of the Holy Spirit.

HOPING FOR WILDFLOWERS

Luke 10:25-37 The Parable of the Good Samaritan: On one occasion an expert in the law stood up to test Jesus. "Teacher," he asked, "what must I do to inherit eternal life?" "What is written in the Law?" he replied. "How do you read it?" He answered, "'Love the Lord your God with all your heart and with all your soul and with all your strength and with all your mind'; and, 'Love your neighbor as yourself.'" "You have answered correctly," Jesus replied. "Do this and you will live." But he wanted to justify himself, so he asked Jesus, "And who is my neighbor?"

WHEN I WAS YOUNG, I would stay up late at night, long after everyone else in our household had gone to bed. I would kneel at the window in my bedroom and look up at the moon, far away in the dark sky. I remember thinking how every person in the world, every race, gender, age, income, looked up at that same bright moon and I told myself that if everyone stood on equal footing staring at the same moon in the sky then the same opportunities awaited all of us going forward in life. There was no reason to think otherwise because, fundamentally, we shared the same basic things.

From my window I could see our neighbor, Mrs. Gilder, wash dishes late at night in her kitchen. During the day, Mrs. Gilder, retired, widowed, elderly, would tend to her roses, have visits from friends and family, and bake cookies. I suppose she was a night owl like me and saved those late evenings to tend to housework rather than squander the daylight that could be spent outdoors and entertaining. There was something comforting about watching her each evening perform the same rituals.

When I happened to wander into her backyard unannounced, she was generous to me, teaching me about her roses and how to care for them. I often climbed up into her large magnolia tree in her front yard to read a book, nestled amongst the sweet smell and soft large blossoms. I felt invisible and invincible hidden in that tree, spying on the neighborhood's comings and goings. She gave so much to me though I doubt she knew the impact of her patience, devotion to her garden, the predictable rituals, and her indulgence in me.

For Halloween she made homemade popcorn balls and those were the only homemade treats we were allowed to accept given the state of concern that sprinkled the news and coated every Halloween outing. In winter, we shoveled her walk without fanfare. She never thanked us; we never sought thanks. That is what neighbors do.

I trust that she is long gone from this earth, from this moon, from this winter, but I reflect on her this year because in those small silent moments when I know not what direction to turn, I find solace most in tending to my roses or shoveling a walk, if but in a metaphorical sense, and climbing the nearest tree, now Kindle in hand.

This past couple of years has brought new challenges with my husband working in Austin, Texas and me in San Diego, holding this end of things together. We have four children, spread out in age, all with very different interests and needs. We love living in San Diego but the plan was to sell our house and join Mike in Texas so that we could be together as a family. However, the housing market is at a standstill and, therefore, San Diego remains our home, a blessing because this is where we want to be anyway. Mike commutes home on weekends and travels around the world for his job, so no need to uproot the entire family. So, that is the right and chosen outcome for us, even though the distance is a challenge, of course.

Our golden retriever, Beauty, deserves mention as she is the one constant, making sure the house is a heavy, blonde cloud of fur. Her joy is getting sopping wet in the pool, aggressively digging in pursuit of gophers, dashing after those tricky, ever elusive lizards, racing through the house at top speed, blazing a comprehensive map of paw prints in her wake. She jumps on the bed in the middle of the night and lounges on top of me, oblivious to my inability to breathe, move, or, however trite, fall back asleep.

Beauty is warm and fuzzy, ditzy as evidenced by barking at her own reflection, a ferocious Cujo at the neighbor's landscapers, and a sport about entertaining herself when I am busy such as the time she spent repeatedly somersaulting up and down our back slope while I did yard work. She will probably not save my life, but she will lick me incessantly until the ambulance arrives.

And, I revel in the happiness of a dog that is egoless and measures her happiness a moment at a time. No plans, no schedule other than hopeful we will eat regularly and often and share at least some of the scraps. Whatever the day brings, she is content to enjoy and partake.

People ask me what I am doing these days. And, I think I know the answer but I am never quite sure what metric to use to tell them how I fill my days. Is it about my legal work, community service, volunteer projects? What about the parenting stuff? Keeping a handle on the house, finances, kids' school, homework, and doctors' appointments? What am I measured by anyway? And, how do I know if I am doing a good job, given that I don't even know exactly it is that I am doing?

As I was contemplating that question and an all encompassing answer, I stumbled upon the following that encapsulates my role, perhaps, or joy, I try, or, at least, my hope:

The Two Pots

A Water Bearer in China had two large pots, each hung on the ends of a pole, which he carried across his neck. One of the pots had a crack in it while the other pot was perfect and always delivered a full portion of water. At the end of the long walk from the stream to the house, the cracked pot arrived only half full.

For a full two years, this went on daily, with the bearer delivering only one and a half pots of water to his house. Of course, the perfect pot was proud of its accomplishments, for which it was made. But the poor cracked pot was ashamed of its own imperfection, and miserable that it was able to accomplish only half of what it had been made to do.

After two years of what it perceived to be bitter failure, it spoke to the water bearer one day by the stream. "I am ashamed of myself, because this crack in my side causes my water to leak out all the way back to your house."

The bearer said to the pot, "Did you notice that there are flowers on your side of the path, but not on the other pot's side? That's because I have always known about your flaw, so I planted flower seeds on your side of the path, and every day while we walk back, you water them. For two years I have been able to pick these beautiful flowers to decorate the table. Without you being just the way you are, we would not have such beauty."

Finding balance can be hard, including letting go and knowing when to hold tight. It has been tough to have Mike in Texas and me in San Diego and kids at such different stages of life with an array of needs, though I relish that we are raising such unique, independent individuals and that they are confidently pursuing their own course. I have carried a lot of water in the last year, not in any particularly big way, to speak of- in fact, in a rather haphazard, meet the crisis as it presents itself, sort of way. That said; may grace cast light on a few wildflowers to inspire me to abandon any restless, typical measures. Ah, how sweet surrender.

I still look up at the night sky and stare at the moon, and with the internet and cell phones the world seems so small and ever shrinking until I gaze at the moon so small and so far away, against the vast unblemished universe, the dance of the stars in the sky, bright and promising of a future yet to come that binds us all so profoundly together, every possibility still open to each of us.

Sometimes the best thing we can do, is the best we can in everything we do.

Galatians 6:9 Let us not become weary in doing good, for at the proper time we will reap a harvest if we do not give up.

Thank you, Mrs. Gilder, for that permanence and stability, for that commitment and acceptance, and for the only popcorn balls we could trust to be safe.

And, as we pause, and remind ourselves to breathe, let's reflect kindly on ourselves and others, as we have no societal measure other than that of finding joy, inspiration, recognition of those who support and accept us, serving others, taking care of responsibilities, and expressing our gratitude for hope. And, thanks to God for carrying the pots, cracks and all.

Sometimes the best thing we can do, is the best we can in everything we do.

Your measure of greatness may be in making the most of your perceived weaknesses, in finding joy and worth in all that you are and do.

We stand on equal footing, with the same opportunities and failings, before God.

Love your neighbor; when in doubt, if you have been so blessed, love your neighbor as your neighbor has loved you.

In reply Jesus said: "A man was going down from Jerusalem to Jericho, when he was attacked by robbers. They stripped him of his clothes, beat him and went away, leaving him half dead. A priest happened to be going down the same road, and when he saw the man, he passed by on the other side. So too, a Levite, when he came to the place and saw him, passed by on the other side. But a Samaritan, as he traveled, came where the man was; and when he saw him, he took pity on him. He went to him and bandaged his wounds, pouring on oil and wine. Then he put the man on his own donkey, brought him to an inn and took care of him. The next day he took out two denarii and gave them to the innkeeper. 'Look after him,' he said, 'and when I return, I will reimburse you for any extra expense you may have.' "Which of these three do you think was a neighbor to the man who fell into the hands of robbers?" The expert in the law replied, "The one who had mercy on him." Jesus told him, "Go and do likewise."

And, the Greatest of These is Love

1. Forgiveness
2. Cherish Friendship
3. Palpable, Present, and Presents
4. Fostering Love
5. Acceptance
6. My Barometer
7. Joyful Giving
8. Courage

"GIVE ME LOVE, GIVE ME PEACE on earth, give me light, give me life, keep me free from birth, give me hope, help me cope, with this heavy load, trying to, touch and reach you with, heart and soul." George Harrison.

For me, music has always been a source of inspiration, hope, joy. I am moved to tears by someone singing well or by meaningful lyrics or the sense of connection with others around me. I have experienced love singing in church and school choir, playing hand bells and piano, attending concerts, listening to varied artists from every musical genre.

I remember playing hand bells, the most simplistic version of Silent Night, at midnight on Christmas Eve, each note crisply tinkling, resonating as the congregation elected not to breathe, everyone listening, focused, the purity, raw, pristine rendition, precise timing, all to candlelight, in the darkness of a cavernous sanctuary, the black of night flanking the archways and stain glass windows. Unapologetic joy, synchronized dance, love upon love, enveloping your core, no sacrifice, pure surrender, blessed honor.

Consider that we are born from love, with love, to love, by love, in love, as love.

We experience and grow in love. We give love, we know love. Yet, somewhere along the way we are also taught guilt, shame, hurt, anger, jealously, selfishness, competition, resentment. We witness and experience rejection, suffering, pain, anguish, struggle. We lose the grasp of fully embracing love in each relationship, interaction, day, moment, opportunity. Tears discouraged, emotions squelched, we stuff, swallow, and eat our fear, joy, anger, and love. Our love is exercised restraint.

John 15:12 My command is this: Love each other as I have loved you.

What will take us from loving to unfettered, reckless abandon, from happy to joyous, lukewarm satisfied to fulfilled, what will be that tipping point that fills us to the brim, overflows, and replenishes us such that even with weakness, misunderstanding, good intentions, but failings nonetheless, we find our way back to the center again?

I remember in college, participating in a dance-a-thon to raise money for charity, twenty-six hours of straight dancing, awareness and contributions for people who physically were unable to dance. We danced all night long, and in the wee hours of the morning, in our exhaustion, when it was just us- no supporters, interested observers, press- just us, as we danced, more swaying than dancing at this point, in the round glass-encased building, the sun began to rise over the snow covered campus, reflecting, sparkling, glistening as light took over darkness, and over the arcane loud speaker system, the dance organizers played the song *Here Comes the Sun* and we danced with our arms around each other, in a circle, and laughed and sang loudly and we were lifted up by God's presence and joy.

And, I felt love, and loved, and giving of love, and present and complete, and whole. A gift from God so tangible that every time that song plays on the radio, I am taken back to that moment, lifted so high, and I smile, and I feel loved, and whole, and witness to God's complete presence.

What is the greatest love you have experienced? The love for or from your spouse, child, pet, friend, other family member, stranger? What is the greatest expression of love granted to or from you? Saying "I love you", a gift, donating, helping, volunteering, offering a shoulder, shouldering a burden, walking someone through, telling someone they are taking the wrong path, pointing someone in the right direction?

One evening I was in the checkout line at Target and the clerk was a bit shaken. I asked her if she was okay. She told me that a homeless woman had made the rounds inside the store asking for money to no avail and then she walked around the parking lot, again asking store patrons for money. The homeless woman became frustrated and after one of the people she asked in the parking lot told her no, she keyed their car.

I told the store clerk about a newstory I heard the night before. A homeless guy found thirty three hundred dollars in a backpack and returned the money. The newstory said that people hearing of the story were so impressed with his honesty they sent him donations of over eight thousand dollars and job training, job offers, and other assistance. She told me that the story gave her chills, thanks for sharing, I really needed to hear that.

Love is abundance, never ending supply, lack of want, devoid of need, more, complete, whole.

Recently, I went to the local library and when I arrived, much to my surprise, the library was closed. Ah, library cutbacks, shorter hours, I realized. I glanced at the hours posted on the wall and was happy to see that the library was scheduled to open at twelve thirty. It was twelve twenty-five. Just five more minutes. I looked around and noticed several people waiting- an elderly woman hunched over reading the newspaper, a middle aged woman nearby, wearing a thick sweatshirt as she sat on the cold concrete bench in the shade, a couple of women standing here and there, a man standing near the door waiting to be the first to enter, and a young man with backpack standing near me.

I watched as an elderly man and his wife parked their car, unloaded a large plant in a heavy terracotta plant, and he began lugging it toward the library, the heavy weight apparent as he wrapped his arms around the plant and moved slowly toward us. My arms were full of books. For a moment I thought of setting my books down and going to his aid. But, instead, I leaned forward and said in a low voice toward the young man, "He looks like he could use some help." The young man looked briefly at me and then walked quickly toward the man and his wife and offered his assistance.

The wife spoke up immediately, with great joy, Oh, yes, how kind of you. Yes, yes, we could use some assistance. Thank you. The young man struggled to get a grip on the hefty plant and pot but then carried it easily closer to the library entrance. The woman chattered with delight the entire way. What a gentleman he is, she announced kindly, her face alight with appreciation. He is a gentleman, helping us as he is, she chirped to the group as if delighted with her discovery. The young man looked at me and smiled. I smiled back.

Yes, yes he is quite a gentleman, I lobbed back to her. She beamed.

And, all because my arms were full.

He helped them; they were helped.

But, more importantly- all were seen. All that we ask in this world, really, isn't it? To be recognized, seen, acknowledged? They were assisted, but in his assistance, he said to them, I can see that you are struggling, I acknowledge your struggle. She, in her quest to have the group admire his generosity, was remarking that she saw his effort, she saw his desire to be of assistance and that she recognized the goodness in his act, in him, in this younger generation, a young man.

And, it was all a gift of my burdened arms that I did not step forward to help and instead helped more than I could have otherwise. A gift to him, to them, and to others as they saw goodness in him and he saw that he could be of value, of service to them.

God is love. God is in us, near us, around, us. We are loved. What better place to find the presence of God, to witness seeing God, in love, in the love we experience.

All we need is love? All we are is love.

Personal stories of love, God's presence evidenced in children, husband, friendships, caretaking, and forgiveness and the spiritual messages and life lessons.

Faith, hope, and, at last, love.

1 Corinthians 13 If I speak in the tongues of men or of angels, but do not have love, I am only a resounding gong or a clanging cymbal. If I have the gift of prophecy and can fathom all mysteries and all knowledge, and if I have a faith that can move mountains, but do not have love, I am nothing. If I give all I possess to the poor and give over my body to hardship that I may boast, but do not have love, I gain nothing.

Love is patient, love is kind. It does not envy, it does not boast, it is not proud. It does not dishonor others, it is not self-seeking, it is not easily angered, it keeps no record of wrongs. Love does not delight in evil but rejoices with the truth. It always protects, always trusts, always hopes, always perseveres.

Love never fails. But where there are prophecies, they will cease; where there are tongues, they will be stilled; where there is knowledge, it will pass away. For we know in part and we prophesy in part, but when completeness comes, what is in part disappears. When I was a child, I talked like a child, I thought like a child, I reasoned like a child. When I became a man, I put the ways of childhood behind me. For now we see only a reflection as in a mirror; then we shall see face to face. Now I know in part; then I shall know fully, even as I am fully known.

And now these three remain: faith, hope and love. But the greatest of these is love.

Forgiveness

*2 Corinthians 1:3-4 Praise be to the God and Father of our Lord
Jesus Christ, the Father of compassion and the God of all comfort,
who comforts us in all our troubles, so that we can comfort those in
any trouble with the comfort we ourselves receive from God.*

He was brain damaged. That much was clear. The way he kept
trying to stand up and his legs would give out from under him and
he would collapse back into the street in a heap.

I want my Mommy, I want my Mommy, he said over and over again
in a sickening high pitched foreign voice. I want my Mommy, I want my
Mommy. I can still see him struggling to get up, calling out for his mother.
It made me sick inside.

I did not see any blood. His head looked okay from where I stood on the
sidewalk. Internal damage must be. At eight years old, I was young enough
to know little and old enough to know it was a serious brain injury. No
blood, no visible injury, and an inability to stand when he had been running
around just a short time earlier. No ability to form logical sentences or use
his normal voice. I was stricken by the sight.

My god, oh my god, women, housewives, curlers in hair, aprons on,
gloves on hands, sleeves rolled up, came running out of nearby houses,

screaming, shrieking, wailing, calling out to each other. Screaming my god, oh my god.

Every week the milkman would drive up the street in his yellow truck, delivering milk, placed in little cutout coolers imbedded in the exterior wall of each house near the kitchen. He was so nice to all of the kids outside playing tag, hide and go seek, or riding our bikes. He had a big smile and friendly eyes and always said something nice like have a nice day or be safe, see you next week. He would give one of us a ride in front of the truck, next to him, and two or three kids could ride in the cooler part of the truck, sitting on big cold boxes and crates of milk. We would try to tell how far we traveled and predict when he would open the big door to the bright sunlight, dropping us off at the corner. It always seemed so far when you were riding inside with the milk and it was fun and foreign and something special we took turns doing each week.

Carl was visiting our neighbor, playing with their kids for the day. There were too many kids for all of us to ride in the milk truck, so a couple of kids rode inside the cooler and one sat in the front seat. Carl and I stayed behind and let the other kids go.

I am going to jump on the bumper and ride on the back of the truck, Carl told me. The bumper was long, flat, and very wide. It looked easy enough. No, you aren't, are you, I asked. Yes, he said. We laughed and laughed as the milkman delivered his milk to the neighboring homes and readied for the drive with the kids to the corner down the block.

Carl waited until the truck had pulled back out into the street and then he ran forward and jumped up onto the back of the truck. There he was, standing on the bumper, holding onto the frame of the truck.

Hold on, hold on, I called to him. Hold on, Carl. I started running to try to catch up and run alongside the truck. Hold on. Carl was laughing and laughing, so loud, so carefree. He was jumping up and down on the bumper, excited at his accomplishment. Holding on with just one hand, taking turns waving each arm around, laughing, look at me, look at me.

Hold on, hold on, I called to him.

The truck hit a dip in the street and Carl flew off. Tossed into the street, onto his head. I ran up the sidewalk to where he was in the street. Carl? Carl, are you okay?

The birds still chirped in the trees, the breeze was warm, the sun shined brightly in the robin's egg blue sky, children laughed and played. Nothing stopped. For that split second all was normal except for this child in the street. Then, he sat up, kind of, and began that terrible, loud, high pitched calling.

1 John 4:7-8 Dear friends, let us love one another, for love comes from God. Everyone who loves has been born of God and knows God. Whoever does not love does not know God, because God is love.

I had to talk to the police and have my answers to questions recorded. We sat in our house at the dining room table. A uniformed officer, my parents, and me. Questions about what happened, admonitions to tell the truth, warnings not to try to protect the milkman, harsh looks and questions about whether or not I knew the truth and would tell the truth, did I know the difference, would I promise to tell only the truth.

Yes, yes. We were stupid kids, screwing around, laughing. No, the milkman knew nothing. No, he would never have let someone ride on the bumper. He was always nice to us but careful too. Carl said he would jump on the bumper but I never actually believed that he would. I told him to hold on, to hold on. But, he was jumping up and down and waving his arms. He was laughing and not holding on very well. He was happy and then he was lying in the street. I really couldn't remember much after that. I guess it didn't matter. The officer clicked off the tape recorder. And, that was that.

My last image of Carl was when he visited the neighbors another day. I saw him outside in the front yard. Someone was teaching him to catch a ball. The friendly milkman was replaced by a sad shell of himself, temporarily. Then a new milkman replaced the sad milkman. Soon, neighbors shopped at the grocery store rather than having milk delivered. And, that put an end to that. No milkman, no reminder. No longer someone to focus the blame on. We knew. The kids knew it was not his fault and that we had to live with what happened just like he did.

Could I have stopped Carl, prevented the entire situation, did I say enough or the right things to the policeman, did the milkman shoulder the blame, where were the parents of all the kids, at what point do you say Carl made a choice knowing right from wrong and he is accountable? Why does someone have to carry the blame? Does it make us feel better to find someone wrong and someone else right when it does nothing to undo the brain damage? When do we simply comfort each other and say we are sorry something bad has happened? Are we left to comfort ourselves when those assigned to comfort us are not able to be comforted themselves.

Yes, God was present that day. And, it was a wonderful day, marred not by accident, but by blame, hurt, sadness, and tragedy.

Proverbs 4:18-19 The path of the righteous is like the morning sun, shining ever brighter till the full light of day. But the way of the wicked is like deep darkness; they do not know what makes them stumble.

I carried Carl with me, and the milkman, in my heart, for many, many years.

One day, I shared what had happened with my husband. As soon as I finished, he blurted out, oh, I am so sad for you, that no one was able to help you and comfort you that day. It was as if a huge, heavy burden was lifted off my shoulders as I listened to his words. I had spent years worried about everyone and feeling sorry that perhaps I should have done or said something different to change that day. But, really what I was carrying was the burden of never having been comforted in that moment, a young child, impacted in a heartfelt way by the circumstances of the day, the events that followed, the outcome, the approach. His comfort released me from that- his love for that little child that was me, so many years ago.

When I think of God on earth, the presence of God, evidence of God's presence, why do I go to Carl, the milkman, the police officer, and the circumstances of that day? What was it in those moments that made me realize God's presence any more than another really good day when great things happened, accomplishments realized, heroes made?

I knew then and I still know now that all of us were connected that day, in a profound and very real way, each of us connected as if in synchronized choreographed moves, though, of course, we would never actually coordinate such a result. But, the still frames of that day, the trauma, caused me to see those moments, much like those moments in the fire, trying to get everyone out safely, calling upon God for help, feeling God's presence around me, near me, in me, from every perspective, in slow motion, knowing there was nothing to change, the unfolding was happening with us and without us, the synergy propelling us forward, the ripple of a pebble tossed across a pond, multiplying on impact.

God is love. It is easy to smile and cheer and applaud those around us in the best of circumstances, when those around us perform to an ideal, expectations are met, and life feels easy. We struggle with love when we are challenged with facing results we do not want to accept, there is a desire to blame, punish, nothing to rectify the suffering. We shut down, turn off, look away. But, the presence of God still exists in those moments of reflection, that quiet contemplation, that fear, anger, hurt. Love then. Then, love.

Years later, when I worked in the Psychiatry Department at Riley Children's Hospital, the employees and clients participated in an overnight weeklong summer camp. I remember I was seven months pregnant with Eric and looked like a basketball had been attached to my body. My pregnancy made me more approachable to the kids; they loved touching my stomach and asking questions.

One afternoon, a very young boy ran across the grassy space between cabins racing toward me to share his drawing. It was a typical child's drawing-smiling people, house, sun, tree, etc. He described each aspect of the drawing to me in detail and I told him it was wonderful. Beaming, he ran off to play.

Two counselors, psychiatrists in our office, ran over to me with faces filled with strong emotion, worry, concern, I wasn't sure. What did he say, what did he say, they demanded, breathless from rushing over to me. I told them about our conversation and asked them why they were concerned. They explained that this young boy had witnessed the brutal murder of both of his parents. This was the first time anyone had witnessed him speak in over two years.

But, he trusted me. The lady with the big round belly, a baby inside. And, I felt an overwhelming immense sense of love for this little boy who had experienced such trauma. An intense gratitude that he elected to trust me.

The birds still sing. Miracles exist all around us, even in those dark moments. That little boy I met at camp, whose parents were brutally murdered, ran toward me, years later, baby in belly, and trusted me to share his picture. He sensed love, he felt acceptance, he was ready to look forward, to open himself back up to love. And, with forgiveness and acceptance, and knowing we can never really know, I can open myself back up to love too.

Love is never offered too late.

If God can forgive us, we can forgive ourselves and each other.

Colossians 3:13 Bear with each other and forgive one another if any of you has a grievance against someone. Forgive as the Lord forgave you.

Forgive and comfort each other and ourselves, so that we may experience every aspect of love, giving love, and being loved, more fully.

Ephesians 4:25-32 Therefore each of you must put off falsehood and speak truthfully to his neighbor, for we are all members of one body. "In your anger do not sin." Do not let the sun go down while you are still angry, and do not give the devil a foothold. He who has been stealing must steal no longer, but must work, doing something useful with his own hands, that he may have something to share with those in need. Do not let any unwholesome talk come out of your mouths, but only what is helpful for building others up according to their needs, that it may benefit those who listen. And do not grieve the Holy Spirit of God, with whom you were sealed for the day of redemption. Get rid of all bitterness, rage and anger, brawling and slander, along with every form of malice. Be kind and compassionate to one another, forgiving each other, just as in Christ God forgave you.

CHERISH FRIENDSHIP

Romans 12:9-13 "Don't just pretend to love others. Really love them. Hate what is wrong. Hold tightly to what is good. Love each other with genuine affection, and take delight in honoring each other. Never be lazy, but work hard and serve the Lord enthusiastically. Rejoice in our confident hope. Be patient in trouble, and keep on praying. When God's people are in need, be ready to help them. Always be eager to practice hospitality."

My JOB AT AGE NINE was to walk down the block to Steven's house, talk to his mother, get any special instructions, usually a recitation of safety warnings, a repetition of the week before, walk with Steven to the schoolyard within the same block, push him on the swings, bring Steven home and report to his mother how the excursion went, get paid seventy-five cents.

I enjoyed my job. Steven was pleasant and it gave his mother, a nurse, a well-deserved break. Steven required constant care because of his mental disability. I don't know exactly what it was. The label, I mean. I just know that he was my age, but not attending school with me.

One afternoon I walked him to the schoolyard, to the swings, like I had every week before. Steven was excited to swing. He loved to swing. And, so did I. So, I would push him over and over again, and sometimes join him on the adjacent swing, trying to teach him to stretch his legs, reach for the sky, and pump, pump your legs to keep going. Steven could pump his legs once or twice but then he would lose track and need pushing again.

It was fun. Easy. I understood the significant responsibility I was undertaking given the somber repeated instructions each time. Watch for cars, take your time, do not rush, do not lose track of time, return home at the end of the hour. Do not divert your course, same path, same swings, same pattern.

We were swinging when they approached, blocking the sunlight with the height of the taller boys, I placed my hand against my forehead to see them better as the rays of sunlight surrounded them. Ha, ha, they laughed at Steven. Retard. Retard, they said. Mocking him, laughing. They smiled ominous wry smiles at him. And he laughed. Steven laughed. Which made them laugh louder. Which made Steven laugh louder.

Steven swinging, them laughing, mocking him, repeating his sentences, disjointed phrases really- a bird, look over there, a plane, hear that, a plane, I think, a plane. Yes, Steven, a plane. See it, over there. A plane, you were right. Them repeating and laughing, mean, contemptuous, sneering. Mimicking his intonation, ridiculing his phrasing, mocking his joy in recognizing objects and identifying them.

At the same time, me, trying to ignore them, trying my best to continue our playdate. That was Steven's perspective. Me, a friend, taking him to the swings to play. To his mother, a respite, a paid babysitter for one hour.

But, what is a friend? Someone who stands beside you through thick and thin? Someone who makes you smile and laugh; someone you enjoy spending to time with? Someone who cares about you and wants the very best for you?

They stood menacingly, commenting to themselves, to each other, about the retard and perhaps, his retard friend. I ignored them. My face flushed. I pushed him on the swing, focused, trying to think what to do, how to proceed, going over the instructions- watch for cars, take your time, do not rush, do not lose track of time, return home at the end of the hour, do not divert your course, same path, same swings, same pattern- nothing relevant coming to mind.

They smiled and mocked, and laughed loudly, brazenly, and Steven laughed, great big, belly laughs along with them. He was so excited. New friends. New friends joining him at the swings to play. How great was that?! Incredible. Steven thought it was the best day ever. A great day. A fun day of playing with many, many friends, bigger boys, big boys like him, even older than him.

The more they laughed, the more Steven laughed. The more menacing and intimidated I felt the situation was becoming, the more Steven was enjoying himself. It was a sad, sad moment for me to witness such mean behavior and such pure innocent joy. Friendship, belonging. Mockery, belittling. All the same, just different perspectives.

And, I was ashamed and embarrassed at who we are and who we can be and in awe that Steven could be who he was. And, I wished I was blind like Steven. And, that good hearted, that pure, that untainted, unable to be tainted. How blessed was he, how uncomfortable was I. These older boys making me cringe and recoil, ignore, unnerved. I did not know what to say or what to do and I felt angry and frustrated that I did not know how to defend Steven. Or, what that would even look like to him if I were capable of dissuading, chasing off his new friends.

Finally, it was time to go and we walked the short walk home. Steven happily skipped his way down the sidewalk. I relayed the events to his mother. I left her looking much older than she looked when I picked Steven up. She did not want Steven to go anymore. Perhaps because I didn't do the right thing? What was the right thing? Letting Steven know they were mean and not friends, telling them to stop as Steven applauded with joy? It was so difficult seeing clearly everyone's perspective, knowing each intent, almost watching from above or from a distance, as a participant and observer. God's presence gives us that- the ability to stand back and see and still participate forward, to love and be loved and see the humanity in every situation.

Steven was so much more than I would ever be. I knew that. Because I could see the ugliness in the world and he could not. My heart and mind will become hardened by the blackness and I will spend my lifetime fighting to regain that innocence and purity that he will hold without effort forever.

Retarded? Yes, retarded in any comprehension of the hatred that no person should ever endure. Blessed? Yes, that he embraced them in laughter and joy and only had a comprehension for love and interpreting their actions as loving. If only we could all be so blessed and so retarded.

The presence of God is easy to find in someone like Steven. He exemplifies goodness and love, acceptance upon meeting, attributing positive motives to everyone, and exuding unabashed joy. When I am around someone like Steven, pure, unfiltered, authentic, I recognize that although I try to live my life as authentically as possible and although my motives are good, that I do live a filtered, restrained, edited life much of the time. And, I want to get further down that path of self actualization to being more recklessly, emboldened in joy, exercising unrestrained love, always finding that good in others, noting the blessing in every other person. Open to friendship. Being a friend.

I am sad when I think about that day. Sad for me, not for him. Sad for all of us that do not view the world as he views it, sad that playgrounds are not always safe havens or respite. And, I am blessed for knowing people like Steven, who renew my vision and wear God and love as a cloak, every single day. Steven, who only knows good, and for whom God is ever present and effortless; love, as pure, not qualified; and friendship, as the potential in everyone he meets. Much love to you, Steven. My playmate. My friend.

Hate what is wrong. Love all that is good. Hold to faith, look to hope, practice love.

Cherish friendships.

James 1:27 Religion that God our Father accepts as pure and faultless is this: to look after orphans and widows in their distress and to keep oneself from being polluted by the world.

PALPABLE, PRESENCE, AND PRESENTS

*Ephesians 5:25-33 Husbands, love your wives, just as Christ love the church
and gave himself up for her to make her holy, cleansing her by the washing with
water through the word, and to present her to himself as a radiant church, without
stain or wrinkle or any other blemish, but holy and blameless. In this same
way, husbands ought to love their wives as their own bodies. He who loves his
wife loves himself. After all, no one ever hated their own body, but they feed and
care for their body, just as Christ does the church— for we are members of his
body. "For this reason a man will leave his father and mother and be united to
his wife, and the two will become one flesh." This is a profound mystery—but
I am talking about Christ and the church. However, each one of you also must
love his wife as he loves himself, and the wife must respect her husband.*

IDATED A LOT OF EIGHTY percent or even ninety percent guys. Good guys.
Guys I have come close to marrying. What I mean by an eighty or ninety
percent guy is someone that you say to yourself, okay, this guy maybe isn't
the "perfect" guy but if I were to measure him in some way, against some
standard, he would be really close to being everything that I am looking for
in a life partner. There is just that little hitch. Something is missing.

Keep in mind, I am not saying that I am a perfect one hundred percent
and that these guys are something less than me. Rather, we are both one
hundred percent people. But, in terms of what I need, want, desire, and

what they are willing to give or have as character traits, there is something lacking. It is a close fit, a really good solid fit, an enjoyable comfortable fit. They are more likely than not someone else's one hundred percent.

And, often when I thought about a guy that I was dating, and I thought about him in those terms, I somewhat dismissed the thought because who am I to judge another- perhaps it is my own insecurity or failings that I am seeing reflected in the other person, perhaps I need to work harder to bring out the best in him, or perhaps maturity and time will result in the fruition of a perfect match with this person.

I would read or hear that when you meet the right person, you just know. You just know? How do you know? How do you trust yourself to know?

Girlfriends would share stories about a boyfriend or prior relationship, something terrible, and I would solemnly nod and think to myself, ah hah, this is exactly the kind of confirmation I need. The guy I am dating is none of those bad things, or is no longer those bad things, or, okay, he is those bad things, but that is exactly normal as confirmed by my friend's relationships. Other times, friends would share stories of a great guy, a perfect guy, the guy that got away, and I would think, yes, yes, another example of questioning and doubting that led to the demise of a relationship. Who am I to doubt or question? And, friends, especially married friends, would share their wedding bliss, the romantic honeymoon, the sweet joys of being coupled and I would think, yes, I want that job, bliss, romance too that perhaps simply comes with marriage itself.

And, so I came close a couple of times to marrying the wrong guy. Great guys, a solid guy with morals, a strong work ethic, good judgment; a nice guy that was fun to be with, whose company I enjoyed; a guy who was smart and made me laugh, and treated me well, and was thoughtful about the little things. A guy worth marrying. A ninety percent or more guy. That is, there was no parting of the heavens, beacon of light illuminating his forehead, no proverbial billboard advertising his strengths, no affirmation that "this is the one." And, I was serious about the guy, committed to the relationship, fully immersed in the deep end. I scoffed at the possibility of there being better or more that I should be seeking.

Then, I met Mike.

The right guy.

The "Oh, now I get it!" guy.

Very smart, huge easy smile, nice, generous to me and to others, reliable, stable, firm in his convictions, directed by a moral compass that was unfaltering. And, he clearly loved me, a lot.

Mike and I met in graduate school at Purdue, dated a couple months, got engaged, married within the same year.

It does happen. You do know. There is clarity. No hesitation about getting married, just when should we marry. No hesitation about being together forever, just when should we take the steps to make it permanent. And, until that moment, I thought I was there and just unsure, I thought I was there but that I had failings that were holding me back. I thought commitment would make me and us improve.

I knew when we took a long road trip and we were comfortable in those spaces of time when we were not talking, those silent parts as you shift from one subject to another, or one of you decides to take a nap to ready for the next driving shift. I knew when I saw how generous he was with others, not just with me. Little things like tipping appropriately, holding a door for another, complimenting a job well done. I knew when we could talk for hours and not tire of each other, when much of our time together was spent studying not going out, when we encouraged each other and genuinely wanted to see each other succeed, irrespective of our own success.

Shortly after Mike and I got engaged we drove to Ohio to meet my mom. My mother was grilling hamburgers and hotdogs for lunch and she asked me whether Mike preferred ketchup or mustard on his hamburger. I said I did not know, I would ask him. She burst into tears and said we barely knew each other, we shouldn't get married; I did not even know whether he liked ketchup or mustard. I told her that tastes change over time but I knew Mike's dreams and goals, his values, and that was more important than whether he liked ketchup or mustard. It made me realize how I truly did know Mike and perhaps did not know the guys I had dated before. Other guys I dated I could have answered that question easily but I could not have articulated ambitions, life goals, values as quickly as I could have said he liked ketchup. As little time as I had known Mike, I really knew him.

We wanted to marry as soon as possible and have a family right away. And, that is how it went. We married, went on our honeymoon and one day, a very short time after we returned home from our honeymoon, when I found myself dancing in my living room to a song I love, while eating a big handful of popcorn, and I don't even like popcorn, suddenly I stopped dead and realized. I am pregnant. I have to be. I am acting like a lunatic.

Yes, I was. Pregnant. That whole, have a family right away thing really got me, right away.

Mike was so excited and would talk to my belly, telling our soon to be baby boy I love you. He went to my doctor's appointments, indulged my cravings, and acquiesced to my expanding appetite, relinquishing the rest of his dinner plate to my growling and growing belly.

And, I worried, what kind of parent will I be? Disinterested, irritated, bored, annoyed? How will I bond with this baby, let alone want to spend time with it? This is a long, long commitment, I am as pregnant as pregnant can be, no backing out, let alone a scary delivery to worry about, and then I am going to have to care for this tiny, totally dependent, baby that needs everything, and I am not going to lose it? Oh, yes, I will run back to work as soon as I am able. Babysitters, daycare, hired help of some sort can provide support. Mike will do a lot. Babies grow, kids go off to school, and perhaps I can bridge that gap for a bit.

Remember to breathe. Now, not just during the delivery.

As the delivery time neared, I thought to myself that I am going to be a terrible parent, I don't even like other people's kids, okay maybe a baby to hold for a minute or two, but that is it. Yes, I babysat children for years, often three and four children at a time, but that was mostly crowd control not real parenting. A two year old having a tantrum? A three year old with a snotty nose? What about toilet training? All of it, gross.

And, as I carried this baby, this living being around in my body, separate and integrated with me, it became more foreign, more obtuse, less understood. I was so shocked at the delivery time, I wonder what I was expecting, a puppy?

We went to parenting labor classes where the young perky woman described a point in the labor process when I would become magically pain-free as the miracle of life anesthetized me, called the plateau stage. Then, we learned she had never had a baby, never given birth, never been close to the supposed plateau she so fondly described.

My energy grew with my stomach and my blood pressure dropped to an extremely healthy ninety over sixty. My doctor said I was like a marathon runner I was so healthy and fit. I felt great. Little did I know that all that picture of energy and good health was just a snapshot of my baby's stamped inside of me and that he intended to take all that energy with him during the delivery.

I went into pre-term labor, so the doctor hooked me to a baby monitor, send me home to constant beeping, and I laid in bed all day, every day, hostage to boredom, allowed short bathroom breaks, nothing else, with plenty of time to worry about being close enough to be viable, far enough to be scary medically compromised. I worked at a children's hospital, saw the worst cases, not a good foundation for comfort, confidence, and relaxation.

I dreamed that I gave birth and went out dancing, leaving my newborn balanced on an ice cube in my drink. I dreamed I gave birth to twins, one perfectly whole, one drastically deformed. I pondered the good, the bad, the possible, the probable, the likely, the improbable.

After many weeks of bed rest, antsy, driving my husband crazy, calling him on the telephone a lot at work, weeks of nothingness, eating a lot of boiled eggs and strawberry pie, the doctor determined I was close enough to my due date to deliver safely and I was released from confinement. I went to the mall and walked for the entire day.

The next morning, sprawled on our water bed, sound asleep, I woke to my water breaking. Five thirty in the morning. Gushing, really. A more accurate description. A geyser of baby birth fluids spraying around the room in a gusto of champagne bottle popping finesse.

And, so, I brushed my teeth. Then, shaved my legs.

My husband asked if I would like a pad, for the deluge running down my leg. I smiled sweetly and told him I was wearing one already, his face lost all remaining color, and we drove the short distance to the hospital.

Then, the contractions set in like the cramping of having eaten really bad shellfish and trying to hold it in rather than eliminating, in some masochistic fashion. Hours of every bit of your insides scrambling to bail or jump ship. A contorted massacre taking place within the bounds of tissue, perhaps some foreign body chopping inch by inch within the confines of your ribcage and bowels. Oh, yeah, I forgot labor. This is normal.

I asked the nurse if she would check me, just check me to see if I was ready to deliver as I was clinging to my husband's shirt and it was soaked, not with his sweat, but with mine. Nah, she scoffed, hours ahead, hours to go, no need to check, brushing me off, first time mom.

Then, I asked to go to the bathroom, would she please disengage me from all of these cords or assist me, and with a big frown from the nurse, she became suspicious and checked me. Oops. This one is having a baby. Much earlier than anticipated for her first. Damn her. Get the doctor quick!

They scrambled, running around the room, gathering various utensils, asking each other if each was needed, yes, yes, this obstetrician is demanding, a perfectionist. Hah, I thought to myself. Good, that lack of bedside manner is worth something, a perfectionist at delivery. I will take it.

The doctor came into the room. Irritated, no less. Really miffed at the nurse's failure to warn of the delivery, his lack of time to prepare, then he snipped me end to end in a rather, ouch, perfunctory, that made an awful ripping, tearing sound, sort of way.

Then, my baby was born, a beautiful sweet wonderful wide-eyed baby boy with a wisp of blonde hair and huge blue eyes. Precious, miraculous, perfect. And, I looked at him, never bothering to count fingers and toes, and I knew he was everything and more that I could ever want or need or care about ever again. I was magically transformed from scared and incompetent to wondrous and blessed, more than capable, with a want and deep desire to do everything and anything for this gift.

Committed, wholly, without remorse, regret, or question. Knowing exactly how to begin and never questioning that I would know each thing needed when the time would come. The most perfect thing I have ever done. The result of a perfect partnership, no conversation, nothing to be said. We both know and are immensely grateful.

The most privileged glimpse of God we can witness is the birth of a baby, born to us, from us, cord attached, then separated, a gift, the baby's soul visible, the energy exiting the mother, becoming a separate being, all the while transfixed on the universe, the world, the heavens, in dialogue and partnership with God.

Ephesians 4:2 Be completely humble and gentle; be patient, bearing with one another in love.

Mike and I now parents, a new partnership, another commitment, an extension of our relationship, a visible reminder of our union, our love, a privilege granted to us, as stewards, shepherds. We relished our new roles. And, Eric was that unfiltered, unabashed, reckless abandonment of love I strive to recapture. What blessed pure love, fresh, whole, from a baby, a child, just touching down, untainted, unblemished, encouraged, supported, unmarred by the fragility of humanity, ego, uncertainty.

Mike and I have been through everything together- graduate school, my law school, his master thesis, bar exam, job transfers, new jobs, Alec's four brain surgeries, wildfires, autism, panic attacks, babies, miscarriage, more babies, financial stressors, car accidents, new houses, moves, my campaign for state assembly, friend's divorces, and deaths. Meaningless categories really, barely scratching the surface of a partnership, marriage, foundation, forever.

I went to law school as mother of two children, Eric and Alec, gave birth to Casey during my third year of school, my fourth child, Karrson, several years afterward. Mike works in Texas, travels all over the world, and commutes home on weekends. And, somehow we manage. One thing at a time. Taking turns, prioritizing. Helping each other meet our goals, reach our objectives, provide for our family. He does not elect to travel and have a job based in Texas. The economy is driving that circumstance. Law school proved a tremendous investment in dealing with Alec's medical issues, dealing with the aftermath of the fire, even in purchasing cars or negotiating other contracts. Not easy. But, manageable when you are supporting each other.

And, all along the way, God, there, palpable, guiding, prodding, helping. Us, hoping, growing, learning all along the way. A commitment to each other, trust, encouragement, lifting each other higher, cheerleader, guide, witness. Mike shows me love. He is my best friend. No question. No withholding, no games, no charade. Strong, compassion, genuine, passion, for each other, our lives, every blessing.

And, we are so blessed, so sincerely blessed, beyond compare. We have four beautiful, whole, independent, capable, thinking, caring, feeling, invested, introspective, responsible, accountable children. Part of us, and well apart of from us, unique individuals, with strong personalities and very different needs from day one. Challenging. Hard. Special, sweet, vulnerable children invested in their world and our world, and family.

Life is not always easy, or simplistic, or comfortable, but, if we paint it with love, it is manageable. Choosing to love, working together, common values, straightforward goals, complete acceptance of each other.

Our children are very different from each other and from us, in some respects. And, I cannot claim to aspire to raise independent adults then criticize any choices they may make different from our own. They are making their way. We are proud they are confident enough to diverge from any course we or others might expect.

And, Mike and I are very different, reaching the same point from entirely different directions, processing information in categorically opposed ways. Mike is linear, methodical, organized and logical in his problem solving. I am a global, let's get in the car and drive, thinker. I make him take risks; he grounds me.

Mike makes me better. When we are together and when we are apart. Better for being so fully invested in each other. We have a playful relationship. We enjoy each other. Friends. Trusted confidants. Cheerleaders.

Truly blessed. Always blessed. Each challenge, each day, each moment, a privilege.

Miracles. Crystal clear manifestations of God. Palpable.

God on earth? Palpable, presence, and presents.
Love is trust, acceptance, encouragement, a decision.
Choose to love.
God grants us immeasurable blessings, some we call miracles.
Being a mother is the most important thing I have ever done.
Ecclesiastes 3:1-14 A Time for Everything

There is a time for everything, and a season for every activity under heaven: a time to be born and a time to die, a time to plant and a time to uproot, a time to kill and a time to heal, a time to tear down and a time to build, a time to weep and a time to laugh, a time to mourn and a time to dance, a time to scatter stones and a time to gather them, a time to embrace and a time to refrain, a time to search and a time to give up, a time to keep and a time to throw away, a time to tear and a time to mend, a time to be silent and a time to speak, a time to love and a time to hate, a time for war and a time for peace.

What does the worker gain from his toil? I have seen the burden God has laid on men. He has made everything beautiful in its time. He has also set eternity in the hearts of men; yet they cannot fathom what God has done from beginning to end. I know that there is nothing better for men than to be happy and do good while they live. That everyone may eat and drink, and find satisfaction in all his toil—this is the gift of God. I know that everything God does will endure forever; nothing can be added to it and nothing taken from it. God does it so that men will revere him.

FOSTERING LOVE

Psalm 72:12-14 For he will deliver the needy who cry out, the afflicted who have no one to help. He will take pity on the weak and the needy and save the needy from death. He will rescue them from oppression and violence, for precious is their blood in his sight.

WHEN PATRICK WAS SIX YEARS old, his drug addict mother dropped him off at a busy street corner in downtown San Diego and told him to stay there, she would be right back. She drove away with his brothers and sister still in the car. After living on the streets by himself, two weeks later, Patrick went to the police for help.

In San Diego County, there are over two thousand homeless children. Forty two percent of homeless children are younger than six years old.

Through the Dependency Court system, Patrick was placed in foster care. His foster family provided him with a nice home with all the typical furnishings including a bed to sleep on, but Patrick slept on the floor next to the bed because he had never slept on a bed. He had only slept outside on the ground or in a car.

There are over seven thousand foster care children in San Diego County.

His foster family lived just a block from the elementary school and they had Patrick walk the short distance home from school. But, Patrick went to school and he did not come back.

Fifty percent of foster care children never graduate from high school and most are very behind their peers academically, physically, and emotionally.

After a frantic search, his foster parents finally found him several blocks from their home in a fast food restaurant cleaning tables and windows in exchange for food- a deal he had negotiated with the store manager. They took him home and showed him their refrigerator and pantry and explained that he could eat whenever he was hungry, that they would provide for him.

Patrick's mother abandoned Patrick but kept his brothers and sister because blonde-haired, blue-eyed Patrick had a deformed spine, caused by multiple fractures to his back. She was embarrassed by his hunched back appearance.

Child abuse kills more children in America than do accidental falls, drowning, choking on food, fires in the home or suffocation.

Patrick also walks with a limp because when he was just a few years old, he was hit by a car, the leg was never set, and his leg healed improperly.

One third of San Diego County residents have no health care insurance. Many have moderate to severe health conditions.

Attorneys in Dependency Court are charged with representing three hundred fifty to four hundred foster care children each. State mandates require they visit the children at least twice a year- a minimal amount and a mandate the attorneys find reasonable, but unachievable if you do the math. With court appearances, visits with counselors, family members, social workers, two home visits to each child each year, travel time, there are not enough hours in the day to make it possible to meet the mandates, although they desperately try. They are paid little compared to attorneys practicing in other areas of law, work long and emotional hours, and are committed to the point that job openings in the department are rare.

I met Patrick on one of those required home visits as part of the University of San Diego Child Advocacy Clinic. I read his entire file, drove the short drive to his foster home, images of what I had read swimming in my head, clouding my vision.

When I met Patrick I was surprised by his soft, sweet demeanor, the gentleness of his features, his easy smile, his pale blue eyes. I expected him to be jaded, shut down, rebellious, disrespectful, encased in a hard shell. Instead, he was open and genuine, with a warm and open manner, sweet and conscientious in his responses to my questions. We talked for awhile about school, his foster family, friends, his likes and dislikes. He had a wistful optimism and thoughtful countenance.

It hurt to think of this beautiful, loving child being hurt by anyone, especially by his own mother. In that moment, I did not want to know his story, or any other story of a child discarded after being stomped on, emotionally and physically. It seemed so unfixable, beyond repair, and yet, he was resilient, basking in hope, still so giving and open, holding to something more than what he had been dealt. I wanted to say something, something meaningful, not cliché, something deliverable, but I could think of nothing to leave him with. Just his positive exchange with someone else's mom. Maybe he could learn from that- that moms can give.

I remember going home and telling my husband all about Patrick, his background, his experiences, how Patrick presented in person. My husband asked if we could keep him. I told him of the many, many "Patricks" filling foster care homes all over the county and reminded him that we could not keep them all. But, of course, inside my heart melted and my mind exploded with so many questions, mostly of how could I continue to face these children every day. And, more importantly, what could I do to protect them.

Patrick's mother made lots of representations, of drug recovery, parenting classes, birthday and Christmas presents, lofty promise predications. Hollow illusory wishes, written in disappearing ink, tied with paper mache bows, washed down as bitter medicine to a young child with the imagination of Willie Wonka dreams. Never fully abandoned, ties severed, as grand plans were presented, fantasies described, though reality presented as no birthday phone call or visit, child waiting on a bench, inside a long stark, colorless room. No explanation to the courts for long disappearances, lack of visitation, classes never attended.

Big boy smiles to her big boy often enough to make him hold to hope and believe. Painful to every witness, particularly the judge, who grants another chance, another thread, relationship life vest. And she cannot swim and refuses to stand though the water is only waist high. It is doable, if you commit, there are resources to help. Your choice. Please, choose your child. We want your success, if not for you, for him. We are in the water together. Watching, helping, holding everything up.

I told Patrick I was going to represent him in court and that I would speak on his behalf, and asked if there was anything he wanted the judge to know. He shook his head no, and then after a minute of silence, he asked, Anything? Tell the judge I am okay and not to worry about me. Tell him I want to stay here- with my foster family.

Terminating a parent's rights to their child to me is as profound as any death penalty case. Advocating for education, safety, shelter, health care for children who have nothing is an incredible opportunity and responsibility. Every foster care child, every homeless child, every child- deserves an advocate, and safety, shelter, care, acceptance, love.

What was he to argue to the court? For his mother, against his mother, for a dream that never blossoms while retaining the eternal optimism that we so want to foster in a young child? And, we know, and understand, that they should not even be asked to do so. Included, consulted, observed, assisted- yes. But not charged, responsible, not sober decision-making that everyone struggles with even with grace, knowing, heart, and intellect because the gravity should not weigh on the shoulders of the child, though we know the child shoulders it every day in some capacity.

Patrick, a soldier in a battle not of his choosing, fighting in a war where there were too many sides to know who sided with whom, would never know where the altercation began or when it had ended, just wanted to be typical, unrecognizable, with parents that showed up for birthdays when they said they would show up, the predictability of someone he could trust, the ability to rely on someone if he failed, struggled, wanted or needed help- a soft place to fall at the end of each day, a place, any place.

No one, especially a child, should endure abuse of any kind. It is a sickening reflection on who we are as a society that we are not doing more to protect children and prevent abuse. I also know, because I personally met so many angels, that there are many, many people who are dedicating their lives, as advocates, foster parents, teachers, doctors, to save these children.

We can do more. Because we are love.

Sometimes the people that are charged with loving us do not have the capacity to do so.

All of us are worthy of love.

You are loved. We are loved. God loves us.

Speak on behalf of others, give someone a voice.

Proverbs 31:8-9 Speak up for those who cannot speak for themselves, for the rights of all who are destitute. Speak up and judge fairly; defend the rights of the poor and needy.

ACCEPTANCE

Daniel 6:22-23 My God sent his angel, and he shut the mouths of the lions.
They have not hurt me, because I was found innocent in his sight. Nor have I
ever done any wrong before you, Your Majesty." The king was overjoyed and
gave orders to lift Daniel out of the den. And when Daniel was lifted from
the den, no wound was found on him, because he had trusted in his God.

● ● ● I REALLY NEVER REALIZED HOW HARD it would be- to write about
Alec. But, I am struggling so much. Each word, one at a time. A
cold, flat, medicinal, unfeeling word. Because when I write for real, I cannot
even go there, I feel myself starting to fall apart and I pull back hard.

God, I know you were there. The entire time. Or I would not, could not,
be here now. But, how do I express it in cogent thoughts on paper? How do
I share even a portion, a glimpse, of the journey…

Do you remember in the movie *Terms of Endearment* when Emma
(Debra Winger) was in the hospital dying of cancer and her mother, Aurora
(Shirley MacLaine), was caring for her? The daughter was supposed to have
her pain medication at three thirty, she was in excruciating pain, and she
asked her mother to please help her, to ask the nurses to give her the next
dose of her medication. Aurora goes to the nurse's station and politely asks
for the medication, noting that it is past three thirty. The nurse's station is

busy, phones ringing, people coming and going, other patient's needs being addressed.

As her request is ignored, she becomes more frantic, trying to retain her composure but insisting that someone get the pain medication for her daughter. In desperation, Aurora shouts at the nurses that her daughter must have her medication, she must have her medication, and as the nurse runs to assist her daughter, she straightens herself, brushes her bangs from her eyes, and says very politely, "Thank you very much."

That scene is riveted in my head because it is the picture of every mother with a sick child- just wanting your child to receive treatment that you know is available but you are incapable of providing yourself.

Dear Alec, my second child, my son, my baby.

We named you Alec Daniel, or Alik Danielle if you had been a girl, well ahead of your birth, not knowing of the struggles to come, your ability to accept and cope, your innate surrender. You were in the lion's den from birth, and fought hard, but not against. And, that is the difference, really. So many of us try to fight against whatever we are facing versus just fighting hard for what we need, for ourselves.

I went into labor early, four weeks early, my doctor was not the doctor on call, and there seemed to be no real rush to deliver you. The doctor on call visited me at the hospital and then headed to mass. I was not going to argue that the doctor, the one about to deliver you, should miss mass. Certainly, if that was needed to ensure a good outcome, go to mass, get goodness points, center yourself, get back here and deliver this baby. Though, of course, inside I was thinking, alright already! When he returned, he broke my water with what looked like a long knitting needle. Kind of scary, frankly, for me and for you.

After the warm gush of fluid from my water breaking and a somewhat non-eventful delivery, wherein you sort of slid out and into the world, a long skinny baby, not a huge head like Eric's that I asked be measured at birth, forget the fingers and toes, how big is that head? No, you were very long and skinny, light, small head, long drawn out but easy birth, big pronounced eyes, quiet. Quiet.

I knew, even in that moment, the minute you were born that something was wrong with your head. But, at first, I simply thought the doctors had elected not to tell me right away, because there was nothing they could do. And I waited, for someone to give me an explanation. Then, I came to realize that I was the only one who thought something was wrong.

You were beautiful and wonderful, and soulful. Those gigantic round, knowing eyes looking back at me.

We took you home from the hospital after two days of me asking Dad what was wrong with your head and him looking at me like I was odd. And, so I stopped asking. But, I knew. Something. I knew something but I was frustrated that I really did not know.

You did not sleep for more than two hours at a time, screaming for hours upon waking and throughout the day. You would not nurse. And, over time your head became more and more misshapen. You preferred not to be held. What baby prefers not to be held; is more comfortable lying down instead of snuggled tight? I knew something was wrong.

In an attempt to figure out what was wrong with your head, over the next nine weeks, I took you to nine doctors. The first eight patted my head, told me I was an overanxious mother, I should take a pill, and get some rest. Many of the doctors looked at your blond haired, blue-eyed three-year-old brother Eric and said, referring to your premature features, not every baby is a Gerber baby. It made me sad that the doctors thought that somehow on some level that I rejected you and expected you to be a carbon copy of Eric. I was not seeking another Eric; I was seeking a whole, healthy Alec.

One inept doctor suggested that, at age three weeks, you were independent and, therefore, did not want to be held. At three weeks old you were independent? In what respect?

A doctor's visit each and every week and more. I took you in for fevers, for crying, for well baby visits, vaccines, anything and everything. At the emergency room for a high fever, I asked about your head. At the well baby visit, I asked about your head. The doctors looked at me critically, and pointedly stated that you were fine. The stern looks were harsh, judgmental, dismissive. It was so clear to me and so blind to all of them. Incredible. It was incredible.

I prayed. When I looked in the mirror, a worried exhausted version of myself looked back at me. I asked for help, in prayer.

My head and heart told me that I wasn't wrong. That I needed to persevere. I was determined to fight for your medical care and had to rely on and trust my instincts even in the face of criticism. I know now that I have it within me to challenge what is wrong.

That voice in your head is God's whisper. Listen to that voice. It is your own; it is God's.

Trust yourself, Trust God.

Psalm 9:10 Those who know your name trust in you, for you, LORD, have never forsaken those who seek you.

The ninth doctor, the Chief of Pediatrics at Riley Children's Hospital, Dr. Morris Green, took one look at you and knew immediately what was wrong with your head. He told me you were born with craniosynostosis, which is a fancy way of saying you did not have a soft spot, in fact all of the major sutures on your skull were completely closed.

We were rushed to x-ray to confirm the diagnosis and then to neurosurgery. We were told if we waited just four more weeks there would be nothing they could do to save you. This was one of the most severe cases they had ever seen, and they were not sure that you would ever talk, walk, or be toilet-trained. You were born four weeks early, one of God's many gifts to us.

I felt so relieved and so crazy at the same time. Relieved to have a diagnosis that meant you would have to have your skull removed? I mean literally, sawed off. They told me they were going to saw off your skull. No, I was relieved that someone understood and was capable of, at least trying to, help you. And, that a weight had been lifted off my shoulders and placed onto the doctors, at least for now, to address what they knew and could do for you. A very heavy weight. And, I took a much needed, if only temporary, big breath.

At eleven weeks old, you had a full craniotomy. The entire top of your skull was removed to allow your brain to grow. I remember picking up your tiny body, bandaged head swollen beyond recognition, searching for a visible clue to confirm that this was in fact my child, and asking myself what have I done. The doctor said to take care when we held you, to lift you very slowly because your brain would swoosh in your head without the skull to keep it in place.

We took you home and you still did not sleep, and you still struggled, and you endured much pain in recovering from the surgery. For another fourteen months, you slept two hours each night. We took turns holding you, rocking you, so sleep deprived, all of us, Eric, you, us.

To fight so hard for something, to struggle, to search, to beg for an answer, to try to get someone, anyone to listen and then to finally reach that pinnacle, to have someone answer back and find that this is the answer was so harsh. To have the cure, at this point, just one step in the cure, and that answer meant inflicting so much pain on you, a baby that was suffering so much already, seemed so barbaric. But, we trusted, we prayed, we cried a lot, we ached for you.

And, we knew, we have always known, that life is not fair. Not fair by any means. It was so difficult to bear. And, we told each other and ourselves, that God does not give you more than you can handle but we added the caveat, half serious, half laughing, yes, but why is it that he gives you all that you can possibly bear. He did. And then more, and then more and more.

But, you were the one enduring it; we were the witnesses, keeping the notes, tracking your progress, ever vigilant. And, we marveled at your endurance, perseverance, your ability to cope, to put it all behind you, to move forward, each day, each additional doctor's appointment, obstacle, challenge. Never changing you. Never compromising you. Throughout the process, I have always known you and seen you well beyond each procedure, scar, well beyond each day.

When you were two years old, going to doctor after doctor, test after test, growing and learning, playing, trying to be like every other child, but having an incredible amount of medical care, and no real end in sight, I sat you down and we talked about the journey.

I told you I did not know what the future held, in terms of how many doctor's visits, surgeries, procedures, tests, you would have and that it didn't really matter anyway because your job was to be a kid, play, learn, grow, and my job was to worry about the rest of it. If you were worried about anything you could tell me, ask me any question, I would always tell you the truth, always keep you fully informed, never lie about anything, but you had to give me all your worry, because that is my job, to worry, and your job, to be a kid.

That was our pact and you honored it and so did I. Always, forever, I worried enough for both of us but I told you everything, the truth, plain facts, no sugar, but no drama either. And, you were the little soldier, holding your arm out to have blood drawn, laying still for cat scans and MRIs, enduring the poking and prodding of lots and lots of medical visits. Without complaint.

We were drained, exhausted, and truly appreciative that God gave you to us because, although we doubted ourselves a lot and felt really at our maximum, we also knew that many people could not endure the challenge at hand, and that if anyone could handle it, we could, and that we wanted to be the ones charged with that responsibility. We wanted to care for you, to endure for you. You have always been worth it. And more.

1 Timothy 6:20-21 Timothy, guard what has been entrusted to your care. Turn away from godless chatter and the opposing ideas of what is falsely called knowledge, which some have professed and in so doing have departed from the faith.

Grace be with you all.

Although we had reasonably good insurance coverage, and insurance paid for the majority of the medical costs, the remainder of the bills, the portion that was our responsibility, was more than Mike's yearly salary working for the Navy. So, we applied for many, many credit cards and charged each one to the credit limit. We charged the surgery and all of our household bills to many credit cards and then dug ourselves out a little at a time. It took all that we had- all of our savings, our modest retirement account, all depleted for that surgery. Some people encouraged us to apply for bankruptcy, but we didn't. We had to try to make it ourselves first.

With Alec not sleeping all night long, crying all the time, the financial pressures, people would ask how we did it- did we think about walking away from the problems, did the pressure come between Mike and me, were we afraid about our financial situation. And, of course, we were afraid. Afraid that we would miss something else, like the doctors had. Afraid that our insurance company would deny an important medical procedure or follow-up care. But never wanting to give up. Never willing to quit.

Don't give up.

Psalm 18:2 The LORD is my rock, my fortress and my deliverer; my God is my rock, in whom I take refuge, my shield and the horn of my salvation, my stronghold.

Maybe we were too tired to think about it. But, I think the truth is that we recognized this was a tough situation for anyone, so why should we be selfish and leave the other to forge ahead alone. We are committed to each other; together we believed we could do whatever needed to be done, and we needed to dig deep and just do it. Period. No conversation. No choice. Not trapped either. Our family. Our needs. Besides, this was just the beginning...

Alec taught me that I can fight for what is right and get it and he taught me that my love for my kids is boundless, that love itself is boundless. He gave me a taste of the depth and breadth of love.

Love is boundless.

1 Corinthians 16:14 Do everything in love.

When we first moved to San Diego, Alec was one and a half years old. We were driving down I-15 late one night, with Eric and Alec in the backseat. Suddenly, Alec pointed to the sky and said God, God, I see God. Well, that about gave Mike and I heart attacks. We looked up at the sky and there was the cross seemingly suspended, floating in the sky. It was the cross from the top of Battle Mountain, named for the Battle of San Pasqual a few miles east of the site. In the dark, with nothing illuminating the mountain, only the cross lit, it looked like a cross in the sky- God. Mike and I looked at each, a knowing look, yes, God, all around us, in the sky, the cross, right outside our windshield. We smiled at each other.

With all that was going on, and many, many sleepless nights, you really focus in on what you have to do and you let go of the rest. You can only do so much. I remember picking up Eric from school one day, he was in first grade. Alec was two and a half years old. It was an uncharacteristically humid day. It had just rained and there were giant mud puddles along our route. Alec jumped into a puddle and then actually laid down in the puddle, rolling in the mud. I laughed and just let it go, stripping him down to his diaper, knowing we would pick up Eric, pop back into our car and be on our way home. I could bathe him as soon as we were home.

Eric was so excited to see us. It turns out that he had won a prize at school that day, a certificate to get some books at the book fair. The book fair was concluding that very afternoon. We had maybe an hour to shop and use his certificate before the book fair was over. Now I had a muddy, diaper clad two year old and an ecstatic first grader to contend with. So, I did what I could do- I winged it. I stuck Alec underneath the long tablecloth draped to cover a book rounder, handed him a toddler appropriate book (plastic), took Eric around the library to pick out his books, paid with the certificate, retrieved my muddy child, returned the plastic book, and went on my way. One of my better improvised moments. There was a lot of winging it back then, a tired mom, boisterous kids with boundless energy; I still wonder how I did that and where do they draw that energy from?

That doctor that misdiagnosed Alec's head but said that he was independent was right. Alec has always been independent. Mike and I joked when he was just three years old that Alec would move out and get his own apartment if only he could drive. In preschool, Alec carried a little copy of the New Testament in the pocket of his shirt. Now, mind you, Alec was not actually able to read. I remember Eric, three and a half years older than Alec, remarking that he wished he were more like Alec because Alec didn't care what anybody thought about him and Eric did.

Alec has always been very accepting, very matter of fact, not reactionary, not worried about what anyone else thought. I remember cutting his hair when he was four years old. He was sitting in a chair in the kitchen and I just started chopping away, not really knowing what I was doing but trying to give him a basic little boy haircut. As I was cutting and my mind wandering, I cut a large chunk of hair off the back near the crown. I was frantically trying to blend the hair, cutting away the surrounding area, trying to blend everything together.

As I cut his hair, I was walking around him, talking about how I had mistakenly cut a large chunk of hair, I was not sure how to fix it, I was trying to fix it. Suddenly, I stopped and looked at him because he was not saying anything. There was absolutely no reaction to my bantering about the missing chunk of hair from his head. I asked him, I just cut a huge chunk of hair off your head, it looks terrible, I am trying to fix it, what do you think? He answered, it is hair. It will grow. Seriously. Four years old and he is telling me to move on, get over it, don't sweat the small stuff! I remember that so clearly. His lack of reaction to something I thought he would find so important.

For nearly five years following that craniotomy, Alec had MRIs and checkups but no problems necessitating further surgery. Alec participated in gymnastics, karate, soccer, t-ball, and swimming. He had to wear a helmet for most sports. We were able to purchase a specialized helmet used for Olympic training. It would deaden the ball, causing the ball to drop to the ground, the helmet absorbing all of the impact from a blow. Some parents of children on his soccer team thought Alec had an unfair advantage. I explained he did not have an advantage, in fact he had a disadvantage; he could not do a header with the soccer ball- the ball would just drop, not ricochet off the helmet, he could not control the ball with his head. It was shocking to have parents of four year olds concerned about advantage versus safety. I trust that they were simply advocating equity for their children.

Other parents criticized me for allowing him to play, letting him sleep on a bunk bed, skateboard, or ride a bike. Those parents thought Alec should not engage in any activity at all. I know they were simply concerned and wanted him well. I worried enough for all of those parents and more. It was so hard, both worrying and surrendering, committed to raising an independent, resourceful child, advocating for his health care, and allowing him to fall down on occasion.

Everyone has to parent to each individual child, addressing that child's needs, taking into account that family's values. For us, Alec had to be Alec.

And, after four boys, frankly, I have found they show up from God's hands to ours with their own personality and we shepherd and guide them but they are who they are.

Then, Alec began having headaches so severe that he would hold his head with both hands and scream out in pain, often throwing up. His MRI revealed several things: his brain was scalloping as it abutted the skull, the skull was mothing or dimpling from the constant pressure of the brain, and an arachnoid cyst full of spinal fluid had pooled in the temporal lobe of his brain. In other words, the pressure of the brain had worn the skull and the pressure of the skull had permanently damaged the brain.

The craniofacial team decided to shunt the cyst to alleviate the intracranial pressure, with the hope that the cyst would drain, the brain would recede into the space where the cyst had been, thereby providing room for the spinal fluid to once again make its path between the brain and skull.

A few days before his scheduled surgery, I received a call from a woman who explained she was the mother of the high school girl that taught Alec's gymnastics class. She had learned of Alec and his surgery from her daughter and wanted me to know that she and her prayer group were going to pray for me, for Alec, for our family, for our well-being and peace, confidence, comfort. I was startled to receive the call but thanked her and hung up the phone without giving it a lot of thought other than thinking that it was a nice gesture.

Well, I can tell you with one hundred percent certainty that I walked on those prayers for days. For several days after that phone call, I truly felt lifted, my feet lighter, my walk at little higher, more bounce in my step, less weight on my shoulders. It was remarkable. Particularly since she, still to this day, has never met anyone in our family. And, that is the power of prayer. We have this device that we can use any time, to talk to God, to express our fears and our confusion, and feel the burdens lightened. We can turn ourselves over to God. In prayer. We can help others.

Prayer is powerful.

Philippians 4:4-9 Rejoice in the Lord always. I will say it again: Rejoice! Let your gentleness be evident to all. The Lord is near. Do not be anxious about anything, but in every situation, by prayer and petition, with thanksgiving, present your requests to God. And the peace of God, which transcends all understanding, which guards your hearts and your minds in Christ Jesus. Finally, brothers and sisters, whatever is true, whatever is noble, whatever is right, whatever is pure, whatever is lovely, whatever is admirable- if anything is excellent or praiseworthy- think about such things. Whatever you have learned or received or heard from me, or seen in me- put it into practice. And the God of peace will be with you.

Alec had brain surgery, to put in an internal shunt, placed in the cyst to drain it into his stomach. The doctor came out of surgery, shook his head, and said that the surgery did not go well. They needed to operate again. First, they needed another MRI.

Prior to the surgery, I told Alec that when he came out of the anesthetic he would be able to have a popsicle. That is important when you are five years old. It is something to look forward to on an otherwise crappy day. I explained the situation to Alec and I told the MRI doctor that I had promised Alec a popsicle. In front of Alec the doctor explained, oh no, Alec has to have more anesthetic for the MRI; he has to be unconscious so he does not move, and, therefore, he cannot eat. Alec had many MRIs prior to this one, all under general anesthetic. The MRI is scary, the doctor went on to explain, terrifying, claustrophobic, trapped in a tube with loud noises and flashing lights. I told him that Alec was in karate, very focused, disciplined and Alec wanted to try it without anesthetic so that he could have a popsicle. First we were going to try it without anesthetic.

Oh, well, of course, the doctor said as he snapped into a much more delightful rendition of the MRI- it is like being in a spaceship, it is really cool, and fun, and amazing. Sheesh. Could we have started with that description, please? I told Alec that I would go in with him, if I moved then he could move, if I stayed still, he must stay still. There was a small mirror above his head, angled so that he could see me. I stared at his image in that mirror, right into his pale blue eyes, and he stared back at me throughout the lengthy procedure. Bottom line, he did it and he got his popsicle. That was all, however, because he had to have another brain surgery the next day.

The second surgery went better and he was released, back to start kindergarten, back to normalcy, we hoped and prayed. He kept pace with his peers. We held our breath that he would be able to learn to read. We were warned that the presence of the shunt could also stunt his analytical development. While we held our breath, Alec zoomed ahead academically.

Spinal fluid flows between the brain and skull to lubricate the brain and act as a shock absorber in the event of traumatic injury. The spinal fluid is then circulated throughout the body. Alec's skull and brain are so closely interlocked that the spinal fluid is unable to flow over the brain, and instead pools in a space inside the brain. The shunt redirected the fluid to the stomach so that it could be circulated throughout the body once again. The arachnoid cyst in Alec's brain also indicated absence of brain matter in that portion of his brain. The doctors believe that portion of his brain, as much as one sixth, never developed.

A head trauma such as a mild concussion could be life threatening. Alec does not have the spinal fluid to absorb the shock to the skull and the brain does not have room to swell. If Alec suffers a head trauma, his medical treatment must be swift and aggressive.

God never gives you more
than you can handle,
but sometimes
he gives you all
you think you can bear.

Jeremiah 29:11-14 For I know the plans I have for you, declares the LORD, plans for welfare and not for evil, to give you a future and a hope. Then you will call upon me and come and pray to me, and I will hear you. You will seek me and find me, when you seek me with all your heart. I will be found by you, declares the LORD, and I will restore your fortunes and gather you from all the nations and all the places where I have driven you, declares the LORD, and I will bring you back to the place from which I sent you into exile.

And, so there were even more well-meaning acquaintances that expected us to wrap Alec in bubble wrap and keep him on a cushioned surface, reading books, watching TV, anything extremely low risk. They were appalled that Alec slept on the top bunk of his bunk bed, played sports, climbed fences, did tricks on his skateboard. Alec lives life with vigor and enthusiasm. I don't think it is possible for Alec to walk in a space where there is room to run or jump. Yes, I snuck into his room at night and put pillows along the side of his bed, he wore a helmet for sports, I yelled at him to get off the fence, and otherwise tried to let him grow, not hide in a shadow fearing what might come next.

The surgery was successful in alleviating the intracranial pressure but only at low altitudes. Alec could not go into altitude above thirty five hundred feet or so, which is quite low. It meant we could not travel; even layovers had to be in cities with a higher altitude.

Later, at another post-surgery checkup, we were told that the MRI Center at Children's Hospital had a policy of giving anesthetic to children under a certain age because they believed the children could not maintain one position long enough to administer an MRI. That was prior to meeting Alec. Our persistence and Alec's self-discipline resulted in an entire restructuring of the MRI philosophy of administering anesthetic to child patients. Many children are now given the option to try the MRI procedure without anesthetic. What a huge triumph for Alec, his success giving an opportunity to many more children so that they may avoid the health risks associated with anesthetic- even if his purpose at the time was to have a popsicle.

A team of seventeen doctors oversaw different aspects of Alec's medical care, each representing various specialties, all experts in that area of medicine.

I remember on one occasion, one of our esteemed doctors entered our small examination room, with a crowd of residents behind him, I guess, important novices in white lab coats, straining to hear every word, acting with the import of someone educated but not yet titled, credentialed and awaiting certification, a company of mutual adoration club members. I listened but not with the same worship. This is craniosynostosis with an arachnoid cyst in the temporal lobe, etc, he relayed to the bobbing heads encircling him. Um. Excuse me. No, it is not. I interjected. This is Alec, he is six years old, in the first grade, and he *has* craniosystosis with an arachnoid cyst in the temporal lobe. I pointedly stated. Yes, yes. The doctor nodded his agreement. Alec, Alec Heumann. Particularly important as this is all being stated in front of my son. Thank you.

And, I was truly grateful for everyone's care, interest, expertise, but at the same time, I still had to protect him, to interrupt, to make sure that everyone understood and recognized the person behind the diagnosis. My job. Not his. Not my child's job.

When Alec was six years old, he wanted to get pierced ears. The shunt stuck up under his skin around the back of his ear. It was not particularly noticeable, but getting his ears pierced seemed to be Alec's way to dictate why people might stare or notice him, rather than noticing his physical scars. I remember a mother of another boy in Alec's first grade class came up to me after school and asked me if I knew that Alec had pierced ears. I said yes. She said, what do you think about that? I said, I don't know, what do *you* think about that. She said, well, I asked my son and he just shrugged his shoulders. I said that is sort of how I feel about it too.

He wore the earrings about six months and then stopped. For a time Alec put different colored gels in his hair and made different designs and spikes in his hair. This lasted several months. Hair and earrings are minor when compared to brain surgery, but, to me, they also point to a way to gain control and elicit reaction from people on his terms. It has been interesting to watch Alec's coping mechanisms and to recognize them as such.

When Alec was eight years old, he decided to study every religion of the world. I know he understood the severity of his medical condition, especially given the number of doctor's visits and ongoing medical issues.

For years Alec slept very little and the doctors could find no explanation, ruling out a variety of potential causes. When Alec was eight years old, a sleep study showed that when Alec transitioned from one stage of sleep to the next, his carbon dioxide levels increased dramatically and his heart rate slowed. Alec's blood oxygen level was dropping to seventy six percent and his heart-rate to forty two beats a minute when he was sleeping, to life threatening low levels. He was put on a stimulant medication to raise those to a safe level.

Just a few days after he started the medication, Alec announced to me that he had his first dream. I asked him what it was about. He said, no, you don't understand. I had my first dream- Alec had never had a dream before. He did not know what people were talking about when they mentioned dreaming, and now he knew.

As science progressed, the treatment for Alec progressed such that his doctors were able to alleviate his intracranial pressure. The shunt stopped working, the cyst did not go away, and Alec was having problems, so we scheduled another surgery. At age ten, surgery number four, his neurosurgeon removed the shunt and fenestrated the cyst and between the ventricles of his brain.

This was the toughest surgery because Alec was just starting fifth grade and the surgery greatly affected his ability to concentrate and his short-term memory. Alec went from straight As to low Bs and Cs and his homework time went from thirty minutes to three and a half hours. But, Alec hung in there, as he always does. Alec was meeting classroom expectations, meeting age appropriate norms, just not meeting his standards and his normal capabilities.

Alec essentially gave up that year of school, allowed his brain to heal, managed the schoolwork, performing adequately, and went on to sixth grade. Interestingly, Alec decided to learn to play violin during this same time period. He could play with ease and memorize the songs readily, despite his inability to concentrate on other subjects. He found a way to excel but utilizing a different part of his brain. That was a wonderful confidence boost during an otherwise difficult year. And, through maturation or growth, his inability to go into altitude disappeared and he could enjoy camping and hiking and participate in Boy Scouts.

Alec's eyebrows and cheekbones are underdeveloped. As a result, for many years, his eyes had the appearance of protruding and were at risk from exposure. He cannot participate in certain sports, such as football, because of the risk of concussion. He has to wear protective gear in order to participate in other sports and activities including special headgear. He must wear sports goggles for activities where there may be eye contact such as soccer, dodge ball, and baseball.

I noticed a gradual loss of muscle strength in Alec's arms. The doctors termed this weakness as temporary paralysis and indicated that he incorporated other muscle groups to compensate for this weakness. The muscle weakness, or paralysis, would come and go. The danger with that is that a safe activity suddenly becomes dangerous during this period of paralysis. Alec could be climbing a rope and suddenly lose the ability to hang on. For the most part, Alec is able to utilize his other muscles. However, Alec's use of other muscle groups resulted in him earning his red belt in karate, masterfully riding horses, working at a horse ranch, competitively swimming, and bicycling fifty miles at a time. Alec has a fierce determination that is embraced by those around him. He has an innate ability to see the larger picture in chaos around him.

So many people helped me throughout that time. Years and years of help. Caring for our other children, helping with meals, encouraging and supporting us, lifting us with their prayers, car pools, extra watchful eyes, showing interest and love, giving us space, noting our fatigue and telling us good job, hang in there.

There is little to no space between Alec's skull and brain. Normally, fluid in the space between the brain and skull provides a cushion such that when hit in the head, the brain is cushioned from injury. Alec does not have that cushion, so a concussion may be life-threatening. However, Alec does not have a soft skull and is not at any higher risk of getting a concussion than any other person. Alec has a special helmet that allows him to participate in many activities that he otherwise could not participate in. The helmet deadens the impact of the hit and does not provide competitive advantage as a ball will not spring back, but instead will drop. Wearing a helmet is a necessity, not a competitive edge. Also, the helmet does not provide a risk to other children as it has a soft shell not a hard shell. Running into Alec when he is wearing the helmet will not injure that child.

Alec may participate in any activity as long as the intent of the activity is not to hit or injure another person. In other words, Alec cannot participate in football and boxing as both sports involve specific intent to strike another person. Alec can participate in baseball, however; he must wear a helmet at all times, not just when he is at bat. Alec can participate in cross-country without a helmet, unless there are so many participants that the risk of injury is increased. Alec participated in physical education until middle school. We were advised by school staff to opt out of physical education during middle and high school as the children vary so much in size, strength, and coordination that the risk of concussion is present by the nature of the middle school child and the high number of children in each class. At the same time, Alec engaged in horseback riding and training and caring for horses. And, although I continued to advocate for him, I encouraged Alec to advocate for his own medical care and his ability to participate in activities.

I applaud the medical treatment we receive. We are incredibly blessed to have doctors like Marilyn Jones, because she was ego-less in her care and treatment of Alec and made us value her all the more, and doctors John Kalsbeck and Michael Levy because they are, as Dr. Levy explains, Top Gun-no-hesitation-doctors whose egos are the foundations for success and we value that competency and confidence as well.

There are people who will help- doctors, lawyers, friends, teachers. Find them.

1 Peter 4:10 Each of you should use whatever gift you have received to serve others, as faithful stewards of God's grace in its various forms.

Alec is healthy, religious, centered, exemplifies leadership, he plays violin, guitar, drums, swims, rides and trained horses, and finished near the top of his class in school. But, that is really the outcome of his timely diagnosis, remarkable treatment, and relentless advocacy.

The real story is the medical treatment prescribed is not always the medical treatment granted because of insurance and drug companies cost savings focus. I have fought to achieve the appropriate health care treatment for my child. The actual medical treatment my child has received has always been outstanding, while my ability to get the desired treatment has depended on my ability to challenge, demand, and question my insurance company's objections to treatment options. I have been fortunate to have the persistence, education, tenacity to achieve appropriate medical care for my child. I am an attorney and a mother. I went to law school after my son was born, had my third son during law school, and my fourth son after. Law school gave me a more sophisticated voice to maneuver the medical insurance system for my child, though I had been fighting for him from day one.

I am blessed to have had the opportunity to extend that voice for another mother...

I was sitting in the dark in ICU with my son, Alec, in the dark after his fourth brain surgery, age ten. I sat in the dark because he was sleeping, which was how most of the day, night, was spent. And, the woman sitting near her toddler, in the same room, who just underwent another heart surgery, was doing the same thing. Sitting in the dark. Quietly we would sit, not wanting to wake our children but wanting to be near, just in case they woke and wanted us for anything, most of which we would be incapable of providing, all of which we would strive to comfort and placate. We elected not to read, or talk, or watch TV, talk on the phone or talk to each other. Sitting in the dark, in the silence, our children, the beeping of machines, the in and out of chests rising and falling, quiet breathing, staring to ensure that if the machine missed anything we would catch it, confirmation by machine, sitting, staring, alone with only our thoughts, worries, concern, desire to help, wishing him comfort, praying him whole, willing him well.

Then the phone in the room rang. She answered; the mother of the toddler.

I heard the whole conversation, how could I not, even if I was trying not to eavesdrop. There was desperation in her voice as she tried to negotiate and pacify the person at the other end. Of course, I could only hear her side of the disagreement. No she could not come to work, yes she had asked for the time off well ahead of time, yes she needed this job, she was sorry, she could not be there, the hospital was releasing her child and she had to sign the paperwork, her husband, in the military, was in Iraq. The hospital would only discharge her son directly to her. His condition was too serious, she had to authorize paperwork, and the hospital had to walk her through the instructions for home. She was pleading, pleading for her job.

She hung up the phone. The room was dark and silent once again.

I am sorry, I said. I heard much of what was said. What is your job.

She answered- I clean the restrooms at a gas station. I am the cashier. I need this job, the medical insurance. I asked my boss for time off weeks ahead of time, weeks ahead, the leave was authorized, approved, she rambled, her voice trailing off.

I am an attorney, I told her. And, you need one right now. And, I am free. Today, I am completely free. Let's call your boss.

We called her boss back and had no success, so we called her boss's boss, who immediately recognized the seriousness of the situation, the legal ramifications, the injustice, and he told the young nineteen year old mother that her job was secure, take as much time as she needed. Not to worry, her job was safe.

It was, by far, the most meaningful day of my legal career. The day I did the most good in the shortest amount of time with the least real effort. Just pure from the gut legal representation. Justice served. Even if temporarily. For that day. And, for that day, could be enough, to cover those medical bills and protect her. Enough that she could bandage and manage the rest on her own. It was not about me being a great, good, or even mediocre attorney; it was simply important to help her in that moment. And, it is rewarding to know that my law degree gave me the confidence, her the trust, her boss the deference to get the job done.

Acceptance is not blind indifference or accepting the judgment of others.

Philippians 1:9-11 And this is my prayer: that you love may abound more and more in knowledge and depth of insight, so that you may be able to discern what is best and may be pure and blameless for the day of Christ, filled with the fruit of righteousness that comes through Jesus Christ- to the glory and praise of God.

Alec is very independent, organized, and has a strong countenance. Alec has a strong interest in religion and has studied many religions in depth. Alec laughs easily and has a good sense of humor. Alec is profoundly intelligent, not necessarily as a student or scholar, but as an extremely adept, thoughtful, introspective individual. Alec is very accepting, thoughtful, deliberate, spiritual, and is a humanitarian. I am fortunate as a parent, not to have to wait to see what Alec will become, but to respect and admire who Alec always has been.

Acceptance is love and surrender to what you know to be true.

There are many stories I could tell about Alec. This is one story. But one thing I know for sure, all my children have taught me and I could never capture all that they have taught me. From this journey with Alec, these are some of the things I know:

1. Trust yourself, Trust God;
2. That voice in your head is God's whisper. Listen to that voice. It is your own; it is God's.
3. Don't give up;
4. Love is boundless;
5. God never gives you more than you can handle, but sometimes he gives you all you think you can bear;
6. There are people who will help- doctors, lawyers, teachers. Find them;
7. Prayer is powerful;
8. Acceptance is not blind indifference or accepting the judgment of others;
9. Acceptance is love and surrender to what you know to be true.

In the wildfire, I lost all of Alec's medical paperwork, tying all of the treatments together, all of the reports from moves and different hospitals. And, sometimes, years later, you forget how much is there, how heavy the weight at times. I was reminded recently, when my computer crashed and I was trying to regain my lost email. I stumbled across an email I had written in response to a friend's friendly chainmail email. Her email to me requested that I answer a number of questions, things like my favorite movie and such, then copy my response to some of my friends plus return it back to her so that we could learn fun things about each other. One of the questions asked: What is the first thing you think when you wake up each morning? My answer: Is Alec alive? And, I remember that. I remember waking for years and wondering is he alive, did he make it through the night, and going to check on him first, before our other children. And, yes, he was. Quite alright. And still moving forward.

I no longer ask myself on waking if Alec is alive or not. He is better. And whole. And, we are so blessed. Grateful and blessed and aware of our blessings.

God's granted us a four week head start on Alec's medical care. Angels praying for Alec, our family, holding us up with prayer. Friends, teachers, doctors using their strength of character and profession to help us along the way. And, knowing, finding, learning the profound gifts of being entrusted with the care of another.

Ephesians 2:10 For we are all God's masterpiece. He has created us anew in Christ Jesus so that we can do the good things he planned for us long ago.

MY BAROMETER

Psalm 25: In you, LORD my God, I put my trust I trust in you; do not let me be put to shame, nor let my enemies triumph over me. No one who hopes in you will ever be put to shame, but shame will come on those who are treacherous without cause. Show me your ways, LORD, teach me your paths. Guide me in your truth and teach me, for you are God my Savior, and my hope is in you all day long.

WHEN I WAS PREGNANT WITH Karrson and strangers would look at our three boys and my swollen belly, they were quick to remark- I bet you hope you are having a girl. And, of course, especially after all we went through with Alec, we were sincere in our prayers for a healthy, whole baby. Not a boy. Not a girl. Healthy. And, asking that question in front of my precious boys made me pause as well. So, I would answer, no, no, just a healthy baby. God knows better than me what is best. I leave it to God. And, they would nod and smile and then say, but, yes, I bet you are hoping for a girl, and give me a big smile. Karrson. Karen's son. Honoring my fourth boy, another son, Karen's son.

Karrson is my son, but, more importantly, he is my sun. He is the light shining on all that is around him. I remember he wrote a poem to me for Valentine's Day and one line always sticks with me, "When I think of you, you appear in sunshine." What an incredible statement. I bask in the sunshine of that compliment, particularly as it is him, not me, that illuminates my day.

When Karrson was four years old, shortly before he was diagnosed with autism, I remember going on a family vacation. At LAX Karrson climbed onto the luggage carousel, twice, then ran under the security ropes flanked by armed gunmen and I catapulted under after him, a reflexive reaction, but, at the same time, ever conscious of the holstered guns around the waist of the guards just a few feet from the spot, wondering whether I was going to be shot in the back as I snagged him, my target, and swiftly returned to our designated area of the terminal. This occurred on the return flight and we were so tired, four children in tow, lots of luggage, late hour, and Karrson challenged every second of that short time in the airport.

Once we had the diagnosis, the explanation really, not roadmap, and started to make sense of things like his complete lack of impulse control, his exceedingly strong need for routine, and memorization of people and places, rules, literal interpretation of everything, no ability to generalize, we said, okay, we are going to make our house our hiatus, respite, escape, our vacation spot.

And, it was a wonderful solution and workable approach for our family until the swing set burned down. Or rather, it all burned down. It, being all that we had painstakingly spent sweat and weekends, every extra dollar and beyond, secured as our forever repose. Not money or things, not importance placed on stuff- just respite.

The swing set burned down. Just a few metal remnants, burned beyond recognition, the railroad ties that surrounded the base, a charred demarcation sooty outline. It wouldn't be such a big deal. After all, the entire house burned down, and everything in it, including things of purported import, so who cares about the additional inconvenience of a swing set, something of such little consequence. Except that we specially designed and installed the swing set for Karrson.

A visual representation of the work and care we put into the house, into making this our forever home, into providing for our children, especially into providing a safe haven for our youngest child, Karrson. Now a blackened heap of trash.

Mike thought out the layout, measured and remeasured, ordered a traditional set, thoughtfully modified it to capture all of Karrson's needs and desires, allowing room for swings to stretch to the sky, allowing extra room for woodchips to catch a falling or jumping child.

And Karrson has a voracious appetite for swinging, spinning, and all related movement. Hence, the specialized swing set. Whether he wants to or not, Karrson has an insatiable need to spin, rotate, somersault, walk in circles, move his leg up and down, and swing. When he makes those movements, he relaxes, calms, is more focused, centered, whole. If there is no available swing, he does not swing. He is also agitated, unfocused, and fidgety. Or, he walks in circles as he talks, processes, thinks. Until he is centered once again. The need is trapped in his body; he becomes manically preoccupied with taking steps to get it, and has to be unleashed to bring Karrson back to center.

The swings had bars for him to flip, swings, a climbing wall, rope, clubhouse, table area, telescope, slide, horizontal ladder across the top, vertical ladder across the side. Karrson would spin around and around the bar at dizzying speeds and multiple repetitions like a trained gymnast, although he never took a class. Then, he would pop off and go on to something else. Not dizzy at all, big smile on his face. Maybe it is need after all.

People ask me what it is like to have a child with autism. Karrson has Asperger's syndrome, on the autism spectrum. And, I have to answer with the following example, because, in my mind, it encapsulates the situation better than any medical explanation. One day, I looked outside and saw Karrson swimming in the pool. He was wearing a couple of pairs of pants, several shirts, and a coat. I ran outside to see what was going on. I asked him why he was wearing so much clothing while he was swimming in the pool. He explained that the water was cold.

The world is confusing to Karrson. To understand things, he generalizes from his personal experience. In kindergarten his class was taking a field trip to Sea World. Karrson asked me what Sea World was. I explained that he was going to see fish, sharks, otters. Okay, he said unconvincingly, as he gave a deep sigh. That is okay, he said, because I saw on the news when a girl got her arm bit off by a shark and they were able to sew it back on, so I guess that I will be okay too. No, no, I explained. The sharks are in tanks. You get to see sharks but you are safe; they are in tanks.

Karrson is obsessed with technology, computers, software, websites, simulators, making movies, space travel, time travel, and all the nuances that go along with each of those things. The computer/technology obsession is much like the swinging. Something is slamming around in his brain, at a strong and constant rate, banging, banging, and Karrson does something related to computers and his relaxes once again. It has to get out. He cannot help it. He has reconfigured computers, created websites, designed a simulator, made movies, stop motion photography. We did not teach him these things. His brain houses the ideas that grown and then burst forth from him, as words, tumbling, and executed manifestations of fixation.

People ask what we do to foster his ideas. Nothing. Tell a singer not to sing. It doesn't happen. The singer sings.

When we were living in the hotel after the wildfires, Karrson began making incredible computer art. The art was so beautiful and captivating that his neurologist asked if we would donate some of his art for an autism fundraiser. We were thrilled to oblige. However, after we had two art pieces matted and framed, Karrson asked what an autism fundraiser meant. I explained that the money raised from the fundraiser would go toward autism cures, education, and research. No, not cures, Karrson said matter of factly. Just education and research, yes new medications, but not a cure. I don't want to cure autism because I have skills that other people don't have.

And, he is right. Karrson does have skills that other people do not have. Art, computer skills, and purity, an untarnishable pure spirit. And, our prayers were answered- a whole, healthy baby.

How do you know if you are okay, or if your kids are okay, after your house burns down and you are traversing a complex system of insurance claims and you are living in a hotel, and your kids are still going to school and you go to work each day as if nothing happened?

Karrson is, and has been, my barometer of the world around me. Because he is so pure in his thinking. He does not understand social morays, politically correct, or white lies. He understands black and white, relays honest feedback whether or not you ask the question, and expresses his thoughts at the instant the thought pops into his head, with or without his opinion having been solicited. He can reconfigure a computer but just recently learned to tie his shoes. He can understand complex quantum physics but cannot understand bullying.

Never blasé, middle of the road, tempered, indifferent, Karrson is an expose in extremes, manifest in the art of exemplification of emotion, raw, unadulterated, unedited processing. When Karrson is happy, he is a babbling brook spilling over with giggles, his eyes dancing, his grin a blinding light of white teeth. When Karrson is angry, he is an erupting volcano, his body tense, his countenance punctuated with determination. When Karrson is reflective, he is sunshine reflecting on a pond, his face serene and eyes far away, wistful; his body relaxed moving in rhythm with the natural elements around him.

He is a gift. My heart. My barometer. He is my measure of whether we, our family is okay, because he cannot help but remark on the truth of the situation, the bold, objective analysis, his observation of the faces and actions around him.

You are eating the Cracker Jack and you remember, ah, yes, there is a prize in the box, that is Karrson. The prize amongst the delicious cracker jack.

Karrson shows love as a fighter jet screaming across the sky, unapologetically, unabashedly, throwing himself around the object of his affection with reckless abandon. He says I love you over and over again, waiting for my response back as reassurance, the conclusion to every conversation.

When Karrson is tender, he is a drop of dew on a spider web, his fingers gingerly stroking his kitten's silky fur, as he wraps his body around her tiny frame. An anxious Karrson is lightning challenging the thunderstorm, his movements jerky and awkward, striking randomly. When Karrson is intense, he is a giant dancing on the head of a pin, surgeon cutting cancer along the optic nerve, opera singer's crescendo to shatter crystal, focused with laser sharp vision on the ladybug traversing the leaf, dropping abruptly to his knees in the street to examine the ant, his attention on the period not the sentence.

In his conflict with boredom, he is a housefly trapped between screen and window, incessantly tapping against the glass. A relaxed Karrson is a butterfly flitting over a field of daisies; his arms spread wide, running, capturing sunshine, bare feet tickled by cool blades of grass. And, Karrson reconnecting is a Ferris wheel ride, his arms reaching for the sky, body rocking, swinging back and forth with vigor, familiar tickle in his tummy, finding his stride.

When Karrson is the world's normal, he is a sheet of paper, utilitarian and resourceful, a love letter, scathing editorial, invitation, performance evaluation, Walt Whitman Americana.

When Karrson is his normal, he is fireworks cascading like a waterfall or clamoring in a burst like waves crashing against a rocky shoreline, loud, fleeting, fiery and brilliant, disrupting the smooth velvety dark night sky, anticipated and unique.

We have swings again. A simpler version of the past. Two swings. Period. We have moved on. He still spins and twirls and swings and walks in circles. We are good. We continue to move forward. Karrson is a measure of who and where we are and he cannot help but remark on truth, bold, objective analysis, his observation of faces and actions around him. Assessment from a perspective of purity and good, his is the one we need to embrace. He trusts in the world.

A reflection of love, a gift. The challenge- to not get stuck. Karrson would never let that happen. And, I am grateful, with a capital G, every, every day, while we live it, each and every minute (thank you Thornton Wilder).

That truth, that perspective, that purity is God's presence. Speaking from a place of love, not judgment, holding to what is evident, trying to traverse the complications of social customs, that authenticity is God's presence. And we try to be present, not worry about something coming up or relive the past, we strive to live authentic lives with genuine loving relationships. Karrson is a blessing as a reminder of that authenticity.

Our children provide a unique barometer of all that is right and all that is wrong in the world.

Psalm 127:3-5 Children are a heritage from the LORD, offspring a reward from him. Like arrows in the hands of a warrior are children born in one's youth.

Blessed is the man whose quiver is full of them. They will not be put to shame when they contend with their opponents in court.

Truth is a gift.

Proverbs 12:22 The LORD detests lying lips, but he delights in people who are trustworthy.

Joyful Giving

James 1:17 Every good and perfect gift is from above, coming down from the Father of the heavenly lights, who does not change like shifting shadows.

AFTER MANY YEARS OF MARRIAGE and four boisterous children, I am the unwilling recipient of a punctured paradigm. I say recipient because it has been handed to me by my youngest as one lofts a ball toward another and the other can choose to catch the ball, duck, or run for cover but you cannot ignore it lest you get smacked in the head. I would like to do all three but I feel a bit smacked. After all, it is not like the rest of the family has embraced the whole concept for any near period of time, nor am I required by some position such as elf or department store manager to perpetuate the façade.

No, it is me that has required the rest to succumb to the frivolity, arguing that the youngest deserves the same magical benefit as the first and that the others cannot engage in the fruits of Santa's labor unless they believe, or at least take such stance if questioned.

Karrson smiled sweetly and a bit impishly at me over dinner and announced that he knows where presents originate, his sentence punctuated definitively. He left the "S" word out of the conversation. He knew he was treading very close to the edge and my ignoring his statement left that firm in his and everyone else's mind. No one spoke further of the matter. And, it is me left to face the ball that has been hurled toward me.

I remember Christmas when Eric was two. We had very little money having put every cent we could muster into purchasing our first house just months before. I bought Eric some clothes at a thrift store and a fleet of matchbox cars at a garage sale, and wrapped each item individually. Of course, he was thrilled.

When he was three, Eric came into our bedroom to wake us, "Is it Christmas, is it Christmas?" Yes, we answered groggily and he promptly threw up all over our bed. We proceeded to have a wonderful Christmas morning with Eric gleefully opening each present, jumping up and down with excitement, and then throwing up into a wastebasket pulled close to the tree. Eric woke us up in the middle of the night one year insisting he heard reindeer on the roof. Eric is much older now and I suppose it is possible that he is not as enthralled in recent years with the stocking and gift from Santa as I purport him to be, or at least not with the jolly magical make-believe part of it?

I remember a chicken pox Christmas somewhere in there but have mostly blocked that from my memory.

There was another Christmas when we went to Big Bear and played in the snow and then went to the beach. Just because we could. We ate salmon and cheesecake too. We had moved to California and it was so fun, after growing up with knee high snow every winter, to flavor it as a sunny California Christmas.

There was the Christmas that we drove to Utah to see my brother Brad. We loaded up all the wrapped gifts into the minivan, pretended that Eric did not have a fever, and drove the ten hours to his condo in the mountains. It was dusk, there was snow on the ground, Brad was excited, the kids were excited. We unloaded the minivan, ate some dinner, conversed for awhile, talked about big plans for the next day and next and decided with two young children in tow that we should get to bed. I stayed up all night. I am told that is a form of altitude sickness. Eric threw up. I am told that is a another form of altitude sickness or stomach flu. Mike was really, really confused. I am told that is a another form of altitude sickness.

Overnight, we left the suitcases resting against the radiators and nearly set the condo on fire. Fortunately, the luggage just had deep seared wounds in the sides. By morning, Mike felt sick. Eric felt sick. I was wide awake and still had not gone to bed. Alec was fine. We loaded up all the kids presents, left presents for Brad, packed the minivan and drove home. Mike, Eric, and I felt immediately better as soon as we descended from the mountain. Alec threw up all the way home. Not such a grand memory making year that go around, though certainly memorable.

But the constant remained, whether in the Midwest or California, driving to Utah or staying at home, in snow or at the beach, the kids sent letters to Santa. They left milk and cookies by the fireplace, a carrot or two for reindeer. We read *The Night Before Christmas*. As Santa grew and cholesterol made its way into the headlines, cookies became carrot sticks for Santa too. Some years there was evidence of Santa with muddy footprints here and there or a smudged paw print- even a magical letter from Santa with instructions or an explanation of where a gift could be found- such as a new bike for Mike on the front porch.

One year Mike and I got the brilliant idea to give the kids a swing set on Christmas morning. We put it together in our garage on Christmas Eve. I woke up very early Christmas morning and turned to Mike and asked, by the way, how are we getting the swing set from the garage to the backyard? We dashed out of bed, wearing our matching red flannel Christmas pajamas, a gift to each other a few years prior, each took an end of the A-frame swing set and literally climbed over the fence into our backyard, heaved the swing set into the designated spot, ran back into the house, hopped back into bed, muddy feet and all, and prepared to express the appropriate awe at the great feat performed by Santa.

You see the difficulty for me is that Santa is the magical one. He gives the fun presents- the bikes, basketballs, and personalized pencils and glitter sticks for Karrson. He gives the cool gifts- doling out the drum set, guitar, skateboards, and rockets. Mom is the more practical gift giver, cautioning safety when using the rockets, insisting on helmets and knee pads, buying the much needed socks and jackets. Mom has the batteries, the scotch tape, the band aids. Do I stop putting out the stockings and the fabulous gifts? Who will step in to fill those shoes?

After all these years of traipsing kids to the middle of the mall, standing on a long red velvet carpet, noting with admiration the exquisite detail of the winter wonderland full of rotating characters and magical scenes, calming nerves, building up the excitement, pointing out the jolly old Saint Nick, hoping he does not take his next bathroom break before we need ours, leaning close to remind Santa that we are not millionaires and frugality is to be rewarded, helping the kids onto the well costumed lap, leaning close to hear the requested prized item, prompting them to say thank you, snapping a quick picture to avoid paying for the exorbitant photo snapped by a cranky elf, usually purchasing the photo anyway because it comes in that adorable decorated cardboard cutout frame, grabbing a hand and whisking them away quickly before they note that the white billowy cotton beard is attached to the collar and hat more than to his face- It is all about tradition and custom.

As the oldest child in my family, I pretended for my younger brother and sister. Why can't my kids pretend for me?

Christmas, birthdays, graduation, wedding, baby showers, and other special events provide an opportunity for us to pause, reflect, remember to take the time to acknowledge our relationships with other people, give meaning to special events, create memories, recognize accomplishment, give thanks, show appreciation, express love. It is important to pause especially when it is difficult to pause because we don't want to rush past those relationships. It is a blessing to have celebration and joy, to take time to enjoy each other's company, to revel in our gratitude for everyone in our lives and especially God's presence today and every day because of God's greatest gift to each of us. To reflect with gratitude on angels, mentors, friends, and spiritual guides. To give thanks for spiritual messages and life lesson each and every day.

Here is wishing you a magical holiday season filled with lots of jolly and perhaps a smidgen of Saint Nick.

P.S. Now as to that tooth fairy, man, give that girl some credit; she has staying power.

Give gifts joyfully, from the heart, freely.

Love, no matter how packaged, is without pretense.

1 John 3:18 Dear children, let us not love with words or speech but with action and in truth.

COURAGE

1 Chronicles 28:20 David also said to Solomon his son, "Be strong and courageous, and do the work. Do not be afraid or discouraged, for the LORD God, my God, is with you. He will not fail you or forsake you until all the work for the service of the temple of the LORD is finished.

I BEGAN THIS CONVERSATION ABOUT GOD on Earth, evidenced in events during my life, people I have met along the way, my children, husband, messages, prayer, assistance, lessons, palpable and ever present, with my son, Casey, standing behind me as I stared out at the blood red skies during the wildfires, thinking in that moment we were all going to die and turning myself over completely to God to get us safely through. It is only fitting to conclude this particular dialogue with him, my sweet son, who begged us to leave many hours earlier, who I tried to reassure that everything would be okay, no need to go.

God present, palpable, getting us safely through the fire. Our gratitude, recognition of our need for that connection all the time, not just in crisis. Our interdependence and relationship with the universe, with the universal energy in and around us.

I could spend a lot of time talking about the aftermath of the fire and of our recovery, and maybe one day I will, but for now, just Casey. And of courage.

Casey was born worried.

Perhaps I am responsible for his worry because I carried him during the end of my second year of law school and delivered the beginning of my third year, delivered him just weeks prior to a my moot court competition in Chicago, amidst the chaos of classes, constant challenge, balancing family and school, the stress and pressure of a plethora of type A personalities assembled around me, and my own self imposed legal mania, between memorization of law and analysis of arcane cases long ago challenged, overturned, discarded, revived, a mecca of intellectual paradoxical hysteria. Maybe he sensed my seriousness and determination to perform well in law school, or my insecurity in continuing my education after kids, during kids.

When I started law school, Eric was starting first grade and Alec was two and a half. I was surprised to find myself pregnant at the end of my first year of law school, then equally surprised to miscarry. I felt guilty about miscarrying, wondering if I was working too hard, stressed about final exams, if I had contributed to the loss. Then, into my second year of law school, I was pregnant with Casey. There was probably an additional emotional worry about carrying him given my recent miscarriage the year prior. Mike and I were so excited to have our third son, but I am sure my anxiety contributed to his worrier personality.

Or, perhaps, he was a worrier because he was a bit blue at birth and there seemed to be a bit of fuss around his lack of muscle tone and struggle with independent breathing. I was in that euphoric state of adrenaline induced epidural supported motherly short-lived, suck it all in, because it goes away quickly, temporary bliss and somewhat glossed over the momentary panic, interest, close observation of his plump simply just fine, no one is saying otherwise, sweet, fleshy baby-ness.

Or, perhaps, he was a worrier because at three months old, on the way to the doctor's office on a late Friday afternoon when I just wanted to get his cough checked out before the weekend, I looked over at him to see the color drain from his face and he completely stopped breathing as I was driving down the road, with traffic all around us, in our minivan.

Eric was in the backseat, eight years old, having just completed junior lifeguard training that prior summer, about five months earlier. Eric was such an incredible swimmer and had completed all levels of swimming classes and had begged the swim instructors to allow him to take junior lifeguarding, although he was well below the age requirement. After much begging, the instructors let him take the course with the caveat that he could learn but not actually get credit for the course because he was so young. He completed every requirement for the entire grueling course including diving down to the bottom of the pool and dragging a pretend lifeless body the length of the pool.

So, my eight year old, lifeguard trained boy, was called upon by me, to race to the front seat and begin his training on his three month old brother while I drove another mile to the doctor's office. I did not want to stop the car because I feared no one would stop to help us and we were very close to the doctor's office but I was counting each minute that passed as I drove, knowing he could not last long without life saving measures. Eric tilted up Casey's chin, opened his mouth, blew a few breaths of air in his direction from a foot or two above him and when I yanked Casey out of the car seat after pulling into the first available parking spot with force that should be reserved for heaving eighty pound bags of onions onto a truck, like I had for a summer job the year I was seventeen, he was breathing.

Perhaps it was the way we huddled around him each time we checked the heart monitor attached to his chest, making sure he was still alive when we went to sleep, baby monitor by our bed to record each errant beep, for the next several months. Perhaps it was our anxiety when the doctor said we could give up the monitor, but there was no way to know for sure. It is just at that point, Casey was yanking off the cords more than it was recording a problem, and giving us repeated spikes in blood pressure at every false alarm.

Whatever the cause, Casey was and is my worrier. He worries about himself and everyone around him, checking for locked doors throughout the house each night, fearing the worst from thunderstorms, measuring the distance between each atrocity and our location.

During the wildfires, Casey was in the minivan waiting for all of us, the first to listen to our instructions to get into the car so we could safely escape. He patiently sat, buckled in his seat, and waited for the rest of us. And, after the fires, long after we were settled into our rental home, whenever he got into the car, he had a panic attack. His panic at school was exacerbated by the presence of well-meaning counselors and teachers constantly asking him how he was feeling about his house burning down.

And once, when they took him down to a counselor's office, when he let himself talk about the fire and about his feelings and then had to go right back to his classroom once again, he realized he had made a mistake in letting down his guard. He now needed to be composed for the remainder of the school day after he was asked to immerse himself in feelings and unburden himself of those reactions, but just in a mini-dose, then stop. Pop open the soda, then ask the fizz not to present itself.

That brings me to courage. What kind of determination does it take to keep going forward, trying, each and every day when you are plagued by panic attacks?

Panic attacks worsened, school anxiety rose, anxiety in general escalated, car rides were not bearable, counselors came to our house, doctors were consulted, medications prescribed. He completed the school year and beyond but with great difficulty. Then, Casey attended school on-line, at a virtual academy. And, he started to get better. Mostly because the teachers and executive director were so supportive and accepting. That ahah that we already know- support, love, acceptance makes our personal success more attainable, tangible, realistic.

The next year, Casey reintegrated into a traditional school, taking medication each morning before school, getting into the car pale and tense, closing his eyes for much of the ride, taking big breaths, and pushing himself. He is the bravest person I know. Every day is a challenge for him, but he does not give up. The students around him have no idea what it takes for him to be there each day. I spend the drive each way praying for him to make it through the day, to trust and believe in himself, that he has it within him. And, I am proud of him for even trying.

He made it through most of the school year then deteriorated, as I understand happens sometimes with anxiety and panic attacks. He become overwhelmed and finished the school year at home with me homeschooling him in things like Physics and French and Zoology. And, I may home school him again this school year. A challenge for me and for him as I reacquaint myself with American History, Earth Science, Algebra II and such.

Matthew 6:34 So don't be anxious about tomorrow. God will take care of your tomorrow too. Live one day at a time.

I am so proud of my child, Casey, for many things, but especially for his courage. I was not eleven years old when the house burned down. I was an adult, and there was still a lot to deal with and struggle along the way. But, Casey was a child, wedged in that space between not believing in Santa but believing in the superhuman powers of Dad, no pot of gold at the end of the rainbow, but, yes, my parents have capacity beyond the norm, that pragmatic fantasy not entirely lost period of childhood.

Casey is my son that always makes sure to give me a big hug at the end of the day. The child I have the sense that will be there when I am old to check on me and make sure things are okay, even though he has his own family, job, and needs to take care of in his now own home. But, that is Casey.

My scholar too, so full of a breadth and depth of information on a multitude of topics, he absorbs information like those wondrous paper towels espouse to take in spills, assimilates the information, filed into multiple brain files, readily available, quick access, and application. He knows much of what there is to know about marine biology, oceanography, including fun facts about sea otters tying themselves to seaweed when they sleep, so they don't float away.

He is my paintball warrior. He loves to target practice and tag his opponents. Quick to laugh, adept on the computer and at video games, movie aficionado, and reliable babysitter to his younger brother, Karrson.

I want everything for him. Everything, and no fear. Solid footing, security, safety. I tried to provide that for our family. Mike and I committed to a life of regularity and predictability, reliable, dedicated to them, academics, work, home. And, you just want that safe place for your children to relax at the end of the day- not worry that it will all burn beyond recognition, that security somehow tarnished, no matter the fact that home is when you are all together. We know a child wants to be free to expect that his bedroom will be there when he gets home from school. Not everything is as predictable as we would like. Life sometimes throws us a curve ball and you make the best of it, even if you get a large lump on the side of your head.

Moving forward, helmet on head, bat in hand, ready for the next pitch, next at bat.

Sometimes courage is something really big, like a firefighter going into the fire, saving a life, or standing up for something you believe in despite seemingly insurmountable odds. And, sometimes, it is something none of us know or hear about, like being really afraid and just getting up the next day and trying again.

He must believe in something, something that allows him to go forward. Something beyond him. Courage is belief and hope that you can, you will, you are. God's presence- helping us through the fire, granting us four children, challenging us with huge responsibilities, providing for us constantly, visible in those around us, sweet messages, painful lessons, and abundance beyond comprehension, reckless abandonment, love overflowing.

If you step in front of tanks you have to have confidence in humanity, hope and love that transcends that which separates us, and believe that it is not just your courage that propels you but a belief that humanity binds you and that tank driver together, such that he too recognizes that connection- and stops.

I know I believe in something, something more- for him, for all of us, today and forever, accessible now, manifest tomorrow. Starting, and ending, if there is such a thing as before and afterwards, with love.

Courage, facing your fears, can be many things, including simply trying again.

Fears fade when bleached with love and support.

Psalm 56:3-4 When I am afraid, I will trust in you. In God, whose word I praise, in God I trust; I will not be afraid. What can mortal man do to me?

Spiritual Messages of Faith, Hope, and Love and Life Lessons

I.   Faith

   1. Fire

        Message   God is always with us and accessible to us.

        Lessons   Rebirth, shedding of layers of the past, burning of kah, release from holding to the past too strongly;

                    God is always with us, presence of Spirit, Universal energy;

                    We need God even when we think we don't, our interdependence and relationship with the universal energy around us;

                    We have the capacity to be present- in the moment- in a way that is profound and attuned to all that is the universe that with the noise around us is often difficult to experience; and

> Knowing your place in the universe at any given moment is any-where and every-where.

2. Puppy Love and Promises

    Message   Prayer is powerful; God answers prayers.

    Lessons   God forgives and accepts our childlike devotion;

    Any glimpse of unconditional love we have experienced pales in comparison to God's unconditional love for us;

    Our challenge is to retain an unadulterated belief in God.

3. Mrs. Beard

    Message   Helping others serve is service. Listening is service.

    Lessons   We have the capacity to serve, give, nurture, care for, love, attend to, honor, respect, provide, and assist someone in his or her desire to serve, any time, any place;

    Our acts of service exemplify our faith;

    Our relationships serve as the conduit to service, as the nexus to God, as we give love as he has asked and as he has demonstrated to us.

4. Still Near

    Message   There is no beginning, no ending, only being.

    Lessons   Integrity, a pure and honest heart, lasts beyond death;

God is with us; God is the constant, in life and in death;

We can selfishly pray to delay death, but death itself does not bring closure; who we are in life carries us through death, on our journey to heaven.

II.   Then, Hope

  1. Hope Soup

        Message   There is hope; angels serve hope.

        Lessons   The purest dose of hope is granted when someone gives you all that they have to give;

                    We can serve and be served. Witness and bear witness. Any time. Any place. Using the tools of desire and heart.

  2. Crippled?

        Message   Spiritual guides point us in the right direction (and kick us in the behind when needed).

        Lessons   There are signs all around us, pointing us in the right direction, saving us from ourselves, reminding us of what we acknowledge we should already know;

                    We are crippled without humility.

  3. Roadblock

        Message   Find gratitude in every circumstance. Angels keep us safe.

Lessons   Roadblocks are placed before us as opportunities to stay safe, to reflect, to pause, to contemplate, before we make our next move;

Everyone is part of our equation; we are interdependent.

4. The Women of Circle 6

Message   Make room for, and surround yourself with, love and hope.

Lessons   Letting go of things from the past creates space for new connections, people, memories, reflecting new and expanded relationships;

We can choose to surround ourselves with objects that exemplify expressions of love and hope;

Recognize the expressions of love and hope in the objects we are granted.

5. 3rd and Ash

Message   Even in suffering there is hope.

Lessons   God's presence is evidenced in our humanity, our ability to see ourselves and each other as one;

When we see each other through pain, loss and suffering, frustration and anger, there is a collective consciousness of compassion;

From that collective consciousness, there is hope.

6. Hoping for Wildflowers

Message   Hope for the future; knowing we share the same opportunities.

Lessons   Sometimes the best thing we can do, is the best we can in everything we do;

Your measure of greatness may be in making the most of your perceived weaknesses, in finding joy and worth in all that you are and do;

We stand on equal footing, with the same opportunities and failings, before God;

Love your neighbor; when in doubt, if you have been so blessed, love your neighbor as your neighbor has loved you.

III.   And, the Greatest of These is Love

    1. Forgiveness

Message   Love yourself to love others.

Lessons   Love is never offered too late;

If God can forgive us, we can forgive ourselves and each other;

Forgive and comfort each other and ourselves, so that we may experience every aspect of love, giving love, and being loved, more fully.

    2. Cherish Friendship

Message   Love as a friend.

Lessons   Hate what is wrong. Love all that is good.

Hold to faith, look to hope, practice love;

Cherish friendships.

3. Palpable, Presence, and Presents

    Message   Love is a gift. God on Earth? Palpable, presence, and presents.

    Lessons   Love is trust, acceptance, encouragement, a decision;

                      Choose to love;

                      God grants us immeasurable blessings, some we call miracles;

                      Being a mother is the most important thing I have ever done.

4. Fostering Love

    Message   Love where others cannot.

    Lessons   Sometimes the people that are charged with loving us do not have the capacity to do so;

                      All of us are worthy of love;

                      You are loved. We are loved. God loves us;

                      Speak on behalf of others, give someone a voice.

5. Acceptance

    Message   Advocate in love; surrender to acceptance.

    Lessons   Trust yourself, Trust God;

                      That voice in your head is God's whisper. Listen to that voice. It is your own; it is God's;

                      Don't give up;

Love is boundless;

God never gives you more than you can handle, but sometimes he gives you all you think you can bear;

There are people who will help- doctors, lawyers, teachers. Find them;

Prayer is powerful;

Acceptance is not blind indifference or accepting the judgment of others;

Acceptance is love and surrender to what you know to be true.

6. My Barometer

> Message   Love is authentic.

> Lessons   Our children provide a unique barometer of all that is right and all that is wrong in the world;
>
> Truth is a gift.

7. Joyful Giving

> Message   Celebrations remind us to pause and to display our love.

> Lessons   Give gifts joyfully, from the heart, freely;
>
> Love, no matter how packaged, is without pretense.

8. Courage

> Message   Knowing there is more gives you courage.

Lessons Courage, facing your fears, can be many things, including simply trying again;

Fears fade when bleached with love and support.

Closing Comments

THERE IS NOTHING IN THESE stories of my experiences that is exceptional or different than what any other person experiences-children, marriage, even fires. Everyone has a story. The point is that I am anybody, a regular person. I write of these glimpses of God on Earth where I recognized there was something special in that moment, that relationship, the spiritual message, but how many more messages have I missed? How many people, opportunities, messages were lost, just passed me by, as I looked but did not really see, experienced but was not fully present enough to capture the message?

Our days are filled with special people, strangers, experiences, messages, faith, hope, love, and the presence of God. If we are looking.

Family, experiences, choices, interactions, love abound, and learning every day, trust, desire to know and understanding, all culminating to a presence of God, that is undeniable.

Each of my children has taught me and it is difficult to comprehend all that my children have taught me. Eric validating the relevance of my role as mother, Alec demonstrating that love is boundless and the lengths and strength you have as capacity to fight for your children's care, Casey teaching me about facing fears, Karrson reflecting back to me the world and who I represent within that world.

Mike, my husband, has made me a better me and lets me make him a better him, my rock, foundation, strength, cheerleader, and coach and he loves me so much.

The message is not about how I experienced the presence of God, but rather my recognition of a presence of God that has always been present, those times that were palpable, particularly notable, and touched me personally. Many more to be if I accept that we are interconnected in a way that makes all our interactions meaningful, if I am present, if I engage God not just when I am fearful or needing but also when I am looking to truly see.

So much to learn from the past, all that has been, so many opportunities going forward, all that can be, look to this day, for it is life, the present, the moment, a bridge between past and future.

It is fundamental, basic, simplistic. If it starts to get complicated, distill it to its elements, and realize there is nothing truly grand; rather, it is purest in its most base form. That we are of love, we love, we are loved, and in the presence of God, with God around us, supporting and encouraging us, holding and lifting us up, we are capable of creating love and being love.

God's presence is evidenced in stories of faith, hope, and love. Spiritual messages and life lessons, God's guidance and teaching, clear, manifest, accessible, ordinary and extraordinary, blessings for each of us to share and appreciate.

I still hate what is wrong, love all that is good, hold to faith, look to hope, practice love, and cherish friendships, angels, mentors, and spiritual guides. I wish all the same for all of you. And, of course, respite. For all of us. Because we are love. God is love. God's presence in and around us. Much love to you.

ABOUT THE AUTHOR

God on Earth is a personal testimony of the presence of God in experiences including surviving the October 2007 wildfires, the challenges of a child's four brain surgeries, another child with autism and another with panic attacks since the wildfires, and the help of spiritual guides, mentors, and friends. Weaving personal narrative with spiritual insight and the unique perspective of one who has been through intense personal struggles, Karen Heumann provides a thoughtful account of the interdependence of all of us and how we can discover that God is visible.

Karen Heumann is an accomplished writer, former Assistant City Attorney for the City of San Diego, and community volunteer for over thirty years. Some of her volunteer work includes serving on the Chargers Task Force, the San Pasqual Vision Plan, Rady Children's Hospital Auxiliary, Rancho Bernardo Community Planning Board, at four nursing homes, and assisting elderly and handicapped adults with swimming, teaching horseback riding to adults with cerebral palsy, reader to the blind, and recreational activities for mentally and physically impaired children. After losing her home in the 2007 San Diego wildfires, Karen provided voluntary legal services to other wildfire survivor families and served on the board of RB United.

Her educational background includes a BS degree in Psychology from Bowling Green State University and her JD from the University of San Diego. She also completed coursework toward a MS in Industrial/Organizational Psychology at IUPUI. She is published in General Hospital Psychiatry and Multivariate Behavioral Research Journal.

Karen and her husband, Mike, have four boys and Karen lives in San Diego while Mike commutes to Austin, Texas and all over the world for his job during the week and enjoys San Diego on the weekends. Karen has met people that touched her in a way that is profound and lasting, whether they knew or intended it or not. Perhaps it was intentional, guides sent with messages, angels coaxing a new direction, or preparation for a future day. She is committed to find those messages and seeing God in every day. Her life purpose is to help one person at a time do something they want to do, need to do, or care about doing just a little bit better. Founder of youBETTER™. Her life purpose is to help one person at a time through inspirational and supportive writing. www.you-better.com.